Ride or Die PRESS

SLAYING THE STANDARD

THE FIELD MANUAL FOR BUSINESS LEADERS WHO REFUSE TO SETTLE

ANTONIO IOZZO

Ride or Die PRESS

Cover design: Wilna Combrinck
Typography: Wilna Combrinck
Editor: Melinda Ferguson
Proofreader: Riaan Wolmarans
Additional proofing: Sean Fraser,
Martine Margoles, Riaan de Villiers
Distributed by: Protea

Set in Aptos

Printed by ***novus*** *print*, a division of Novus Holdings

First published by Ride or Die Press

2025 First edition, first impression

ISBN: 978-1-0370-8638-0 (Print)
ISBN: 978-1-990973-98-7 (ePub)

To Nicole

You've never asked for the spotlight, but you've carried its weight. You've walked with me through every high and every low, never flinching. You've never stepped away, even when the path was steep, even when I wasn't easy to follow. You've stood by me through the darkest chapters: the crash, the recovery, the quiet battles no one saw. When the noise got loud, you stayed steady. When the burden got heavy, you helped me carry it without ever asking for credit.

This book may have my name on the cover, but you are written between every line. Your strength made space for mine. Your belief held me up when I started to doubt my own. Your love gave me the safety to rebuild and the clarity to lead.

As I bring this journey to a close, I want you to know that I see you. I honour you and I'm building a life, a legacy and a standard that you can be proud of. Thank you for standing beside me, even when it would've been easier to stand back. You are, and always will be, the foundation beneath everything I build.

With all my love,

Antonio

Contents

PART III
CULTURE & ENERGY: WHY IT MATTERS

PART IV
SCALING, LEGACY & IMPACT

PART V
EXPANSION & EXPOSURE

FOREWORD

Comfort is a silent killer. It doesn't announce itself. It doesn't blow things up. It seeps in, softly, quietly, while you're still convincing yourself you're winning.

I wrote *Slaying the Standard* because I've had enough of mediocrity, enough of watching average paraded as excellence, enough of leaders chasing hype instead of building foundations that actually last.

This isn't just another business book packed with buzzwords and borrowed wisdom. It's a direct challenge to you, your teams and the standards you might be tolerating. It's not about platitudes; it's about performance. It's not about motivation but about mastery.

This book is for all those who sense that they are capable of more, especially founders who have hit a ceiling, leaders who have become lost in performance theatre and high performers who might be stuck in cruise control. It's for those who feel trapped by the very systems they've built – systems that once served them but now suffocate them.

None of this is theory. I have lived every word in these pages. Over the years, I've built a multibillion-rand insurance business, Africa's first six-star fitness facility, an award-winning rooftop restaurant, a leading property development company and a motorsport team that competes across Europe. But behind every venture, there's been a war on doubt, distraction, dysfunction and even, at one point, addiction.

In 2018, a high-speed motorcycle crash shattered my spine. The doctors told me I should have been paralysed. But I did more than walk – I built. While silently battling a debilitating opioid addiction, I expanded companies, led teams and scaled ventures.

On the outside, I was thriving. Inside, I was unravelling. That season taught me something no boardroom ever could: standards are survival. When everything in me wanted to give up, the standards I had hardcoded into my life were all that kept me from collapsing.

Slaying the Standard distils what I've learned into seven non-negotiables: standards, systems, rhythm, alignment, ownership, clarity and builders. Each chapter is designed to be short, punchy and built for execution: no fluff, no noise, just real frameworks, battle-tested insights and tools you can use immediately.

By the end of the book, you'll know how to sharpen execution, systemise leadership, and scale with precision. You'll learn how to build cultures that defend your standard, engineer emotional brand energy, and lead without ego. Most importantly, you'll discover how to create something exceptional, without losing yourself in the process.

So, if you're tired of managing chaos, if you're done chasing growth at the cost of greatness, and if you're ready to raise the bar across every part of your life and business, this book is for you. And if you've already built something great, good. Let this book push you further, because *Slaying the Standard* isn't just about doing better, it's about leading in a way that makes "better" permanent.

You don't need another business book.

You need a new standard.

Let's begin.

Antonio Iozzo

INTRODUCTION

The gym was dark and cold. I stood alone in the centre of the massive empty space. The air smelled of iron and rubber. No lights were on. No music played. Just silence, concrete and the sound of my breath. It was early, earlier than usual, before the birds had even begun to sing.

For a moment, I felt the weight of everything I had built – and everything I still had not. I grabbed the pull-up bar, not to train but to think. To breathe. Because even after building multiple businesses, rebranding entire organisations, expanding into new industries and slaying a five-year opioid addiction, one question still lingered: What kind of leader do I want to become now?

It's a question every builder eventually faces. After the momentum fades, after the crisis is over and survival mode ends, who are you, really, as a leader?

That morning, in the stillness of that cold gym, I realised I wasn't chasing success any more. I was choosing standards – and not just for my fitness company, my insurance group or my rooftop restaurant. I was choosing the standard for how I would lead, how I would build and what I would protect in the future when no one else was watching. That's when the idea for this book was born.

From the beginning, I knew this wasn't going to be a memoir. I didn't want to list all my achievements or recycle stories from a highlight reel. I believe in moving forward, not living in the rear view. What I wanted was something real. Something built to serve. Something that would meet builders where they were – not with theory but with tools. This had to be a book for those who were building or wanted to build something exceptional, doing so with clarity, systems and execution.

As I stood in that empty gym, the title came to me with absolute certainty: *Slaying the Standard*. Because in my world, this phrase isn't just some meaningless motto. It's a way of operating – a mindset, a muscle and a system – that has evolved through every business I have ever built and every failure I have ever endured.

Once I started writing, I quickly realised that every lesson I wanted to share was anchored in what I now call The Standard System™ – a framework built on seven non-negotiables: standards, systems, rhythm, alignment, ownership, clarity and builders.

At the peak of the system you'll find **Vision**, a directional force supported by five operational pillars – execution, culture, systems, scale and impact -- that shape how I lead, execute and scale.

In my experience, most people don't fail because they aim too high. They fail because they tolerate too much or aim too low. They compromise. They settle. And eventually, they stop building for excellence and start surviving for safety.

This book is about rejecting that mindset. It's about leading sharper, executing cleaner and building stronger. It's about setting a standard that cuts through noise and mediocrity and about introducing and embedding systems that work – consistently. It is about designing a culture that lasts, leading without ego and taking ownership of what you build, not with hype but with precision.

Everything you read in this book is anchored in The Standard System™, the framework that has shaped how I build, scale and lead. You'll see it running through every chapter, whether I'm speaking about brand, operations, culture, setbacks or growth. This is not an abstract book. It is tactical, practical and battle-tested.

Inside, you'll find systems that scale, habits that sharpen, audits that expose blind spots, cultural blueprints, execution principles, stories from the trenches and the hard questions most leaders avoid.

You can read this book from start to finish or one chapter at a time. At the end of each chapter, you'll find a section called "Raise the Standard" – a set of reflective questions and prompts designed to help you apply the principle immediately. Highlight it, share it and train from it, but most importantly, use it. Because *Slaying the Standard* only works if you work it. So, if you are ready to lead with intent, build with precision and protect what truly matters, then come with me. Let us slay the standard together.

Because once you do, you will never lead the same way again.

THE STANDARD SYSTEM™

A framework for builders who refuse to settle

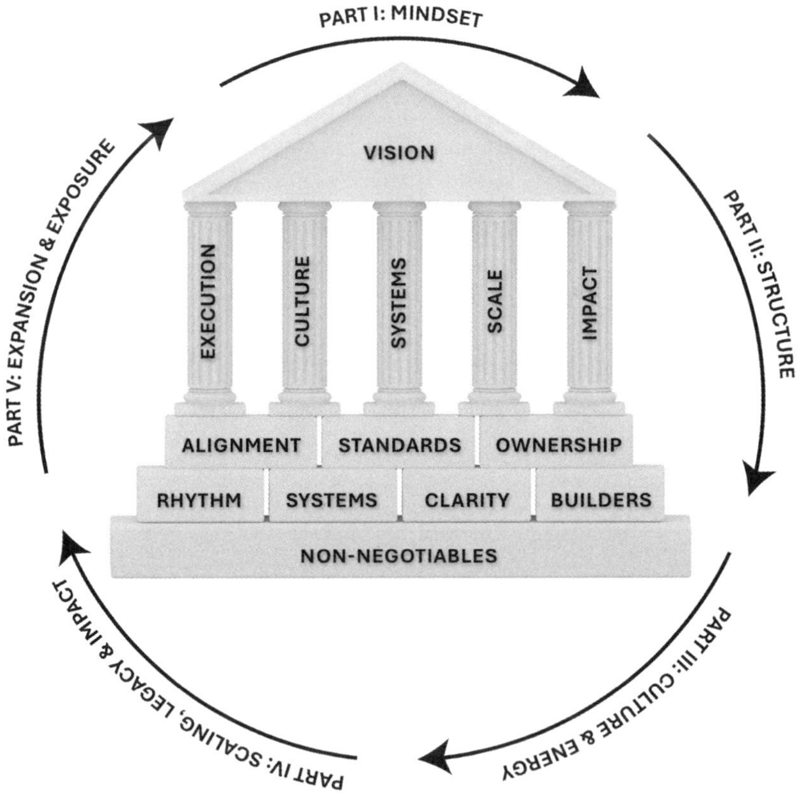

The Structure

The Standard System™ is the structural philosophy that underpins this book. It codifies the systems, disciplines and leadership architecture I have forged through trial, error and execution, now structured to allow others to build with clarity from the start.

This framework is built from the inside out. It begins with unshakable principles, rises through executional mastery and is anchored at its peak by clear, ego-free vision. Every element of the system is designed to drive trust, performance and alignment, whether you're building a team, a brand or a legacy.

The Apex: Vision

At the peak of the system sits **Vision**, the directional force that aligns all thinking, execution and decision-making. **Vision** is not a slogan. It is an operating anchor. It brings purpose to process, clarity to teams and discipline to growth. In this framework, **Vision** is protected above all else. When **Vision** drifts, everything else collapses beneath it.

The Five Pillars

The five load-bearing disciplines beneath **Vision**, each crucial to executional stability, are:

- **Execution:** Finish what others only start.
- **Culture:** Build what cannot be copied.
- **Systems:** Design for freedom, not for firefighting.
- **Scale:** Multiply momentum without losing the mission.
- **Impact:** Make growth meaningful beyond numbers.

Note: "Systems" appears as both a foundational non-negotiable and a core pillar. This is intentional. At the foundation, it reflects the discipline of systemising repeatable actions. As a pillar, it represents the strategic execution of scalable infrastructure across the business.

These pillars do not stand alone. They are all powered by foundational non-negotiables that determine their strength, repeatability and long-term viability.

The Foundation: Seven Non-Negotiables

This system does not rest on values but on enforced behaviours. The following seven disciplines form the base of the structure. If they are weak, everything above them begins to shake.

- **Alignment**: Strategy only works when teams move together.
- **Standards**: What you tolerate becomes your culture.
- **Ownership**: Shared responsibility is no responsibility.
- **Rhythm**: Cadence creates consistency.
- **Systems**: What repeats must be systemised.
- **Clarity**: Confusion is friction.
- **Builders**: Scale is not systems; it's the people who evolve them.

These are not ideals. They are operational laws.

The Evolutionary Rings: The five parts of building

Encircling the structure is a five-part journey that every builder must take repeatedly to grow without eroding what has made them great.

- **Part I:** Mindset: The Internal Standard
- **Part II:** Structure: Build What Lasts
- **Part III:** Culture & Energy: Why it Matters
- **Part IV:** Scaling, Legacy & Impact
- **Part V:** Expansion & Exposure

This is not a sequence. It is a cycle that you repeat as you rise.

Application

The Standard System™ is designed to be used.

It's a lens for diagnosing what's slipping, a structure for building what matters and a language for leading teams, clients and companies with integrity. Whether you're launching, scaling, recovering or redefining, the system remains the same.

You don't rise by improvising. You rise by operating at standard.

How to Use This Book: Icon Reference Guide

This book is designed to be used, not just read. These icons will help you navigate with intention, reflect more deeply and apply what matters most.

Content & Insight Icons

Used inside chapters to signal distinct types of insight or application.

ICON	LABEL	DESCRIPTION
	STRATEGIC INSIGHT	Key ideas, sharp lessons or realisations gained from building, leading and scaling.
	THE MOMENT IT HIT ME	A breakthrough moment or emotional turning point that shaped my leadership.
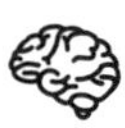	MINDSET PRINCIPLE	Mental frameworks that shape how elite leaders think, decide and operate.
	FRAMEWORK/ PLAYBOOK	Tools, models or systems that translate theory into step-by-step action.
	WARNING SIGN	What happens when the principle is ignored – hidden costs, leadership drift and missed signals.
	WHAT I TELL MY TEAMS	Leadership phrases, mantras and cultural messages used across my companies.

	FIELD NOTES	Tactical takeaways, principles and insights built for execution.
	BEHIND THE CHAPTER	The story or context behind why the chapter exists and why it matters.
	RAISE THE STANDARD	Reflective questions and prompts to help you apply the lesson immediately.

System & Navigation Icons

Used in recap sections to guide reflection, summarise insights and close with a shift.

ICON	LABEL	DESCRIPTION
	PART RECAP	Opens each recap section with a summary of the section's theme and how it fits into The Standard System™.
	WHAT YOU'VE JUST MASTERED	Recaps key chapter-by-chapter takeaways so you can consolidate insights and connect the dots.
	AUDIT TOOL	Questions for strategic reflection as you assess the alignment between your current execution and your intended standard.
	THE SHIFT	Captures the mindset and operational transformation you should now be ready to make – a summary pivot point to close the recap.

PART I

MINDSET: THE INTERNAL STANDARD

CHAPTER 1

STRIVE FOR PERFECTION, KNOWING YOU'LL NEVER ACHIEVE IT

The pursuit of perfection is not about flawlessness; it's about refusing to tolerate average.

STRATEGIC INSIGHT

"Perfection is impossible, but the pursuit of it is where everything changes."

This principle has shaped everything I've ever built: from how systems run across my companies, to switching on the lights at the gym at 4:30am, or to how a guest is greeted at my rooftop restaurant. It's not about obsession. It's about intentionality.

It shows up in how we onboard brokers in my insurance company, how we train in the health and wellness business and how we plate food at the restaurant. There's discipline behind every design.

I didn't learn this concept in a boardroom or from a book. I learned it from failing in public. I learned it the hard way, facing my demons in front of my executive team and speaking openly in the media about my opioid addiction. I learned it from building businesses when I was naive, from finishing projects even when they broke down and from refusing to accept "good enough" and still watching things fall apart. I learned it from getting back up and doing it over and over again, in pursuit not of perfection but of something exceptional.

THE MOMENT IT HIT ME: OBSESSION SETS THE STANDARD

I once obsessed over a single newsletter. I rewrote it 25 times because something about it just didn't feel right. This wasn't about ego; it was about standards. I grilled my staff over everything, from sloppy fonts to lazy customer responses. My attitude was simple: do it right the first time or do it again.

My preoccupation with detail comes from a core belief: everything we put into the world carries our name. Mediocrity is never an option.

I honed this attitude in construction many years ago, checking how ceilings joined with walls, how windows sat in frames and whether the tiles aligned. Because if you don't pay attention to the small details at the start, you're delusional to think you can fix them later. One small oversight always leads to another. Correcting the first mistake reveals the next. But if you ignore them, those seemingly tiny flaws start adding up.

This is the essence of my philosophy: striving for perfection, knowing I will never achieve it. This is not a call for unrealistic ideals. It's a commitment to relentless refinement. Every letter, floor plan and process – I scrutinise it all. It's the thread that runs through all my businesses. Perfection is not the goal. It's the pursuit of it that creates excellence.

Your standard isn't what you say; it's what you approve, what you permit and what you let slide. And if you start lowering it – even just once – it becomes easier to lower it again.

🛠 FRAMEWORK/PLAYBOOK: TWO DRIVERS OF EXECUTION

Attention to Detail

Excellence lives in the invisible. Most people don't notice how the lighting shifts at the gym between the cardio and strength zones. I do. Because that shift tells the brain: *Now we train.*

The more intentional your details, the more magnetic your experience becomes. Details don't just make things better; they make them unforgettable.

Finish What You Start

The world is full of half-built brands, half-trained teams and half-launched ideas. Discipline is forged in the quiet moments, when no one is clapping, when the mood is gone, when it's just you in the room – and the standard you refuse to compromise.

🧠 MINDSET PRINCIPLE: PERFECTION ISN'T THE GOAL – PROGRESS IS

The pursuit of perfection often disguises fear. It becomes delay dressed up as discipline. I've seen leaders hold back launches, endlessly polishing details and hiding behind the idea that "it's not ready". But that's not excellence – it's hesitation with a better wardrobe.

Perfection tells you to wait for the perfect time, the perfect design, the perfect conditions, but waiting erodes momentum.

The builders who win aren't the ones who wait – they're the ones who move. They launch at 95% and refine in motion.

This is where the principle of Kaizen became my anchor. In Japanese, it means continuous improvement – small, daily upgrades that compound into something exceptional. Even a 1% shift, applied consistently, changes everything.

We apply this in all my businesses: in training, onboarding, how we plate food, how we write emails, and how we deliver service. Because if it's not improving, it's decaying.

Perfection isn't an isolated achievement. It's a rhythm. You test, you learn, you upgrade. You don't chase perfection to delay – you chase it to sharpen.

(There's a fine line between perfectionism and paralysis, one we unpack fully in Chapter 5.)

⚠ WARNING SIGN: THE TRAP OF "GOOD ENOUGH"

"Good enough" works – until it doesn't. You can run a business at 80%. You can get by with delivering average service. But that 20% you've neglected? It compounds. It shows up in unseen ways: staff turnover, subtle brand drift, client disengagement, and leaders who lose pride in what they are building.

Worse, the pursuit of perfection can disguise itself as discipline, while breeding hesitation. Some leaders don't ever move forward because they're always waiting for "ready". But waiting doesn't guarantee excellence. Instead, it guarantees stagnation.

Small compromises become cultural habits, and over-polishing becomes something I like to call "perfection paralysis". By the time you notice the drift, the damage is already done. We don't have to wait to be great. We move until we are. Because those who succeed, launch. They learn in motion. They refine under fire.

💬 WHAT I TELL MY TEAMS

- "Precision over pressure."
- "If your name is on it, your standard is in it."
- "Trust is built through the details that no one sees but everyone feels."
- "You don't need to be perfect, but you'd better move like you're aiming for it."

✍ FIELD NOTES

- Perfection isn't the goal. Precision is.
- What you tolerate quietly compounds loudly.
- The invisible 1% is the difference between pride and regret.
- You don't build trust by starting strong; you build it by finishing sharp.
- Every detail is a signal. If you don't see it, your customer still feels it.
- The gap between "almost right" and exceptional is where trust, loyalty and legacy are built.

🔍 BEHIND THE CHAPTER

This principle didn't come from theory. It came from pressure. I didn't write this chapter because I wanted to sound "disciplined". I wrote it because I've seen what happens when you lower your standards. In my experience, when your business grows fast, the pressure to move quickly often forces you to cut corners and sign off on things that are just "good enough". I've done it. I've approved campaigns I wasn't proud of. I've let the bar slip to meet a deadline. I've launched before we were ready, and I regretted it. But I've also seen what it feels like to walk into a space and think, "We've nailed this." To look at a document or a pitch deck and feel, "This is the standard. This is us."

This chapter is about drawing a personal line in the sand – not because I've mastered perfection but because I've experienced the cost of ignoring it.

RAISE THE STANDARD

- What standard needs to be raised today?
- Where did you let something slide yesterday?
- Who or what needs to feel the elevation today?
- Where in your life or business are you tolerating "almost right"?
- What detail, process or behaviour could you improve by just 1% every day?

In the next chapter, we shift from high standards to hidden signals and explore why excellence lives in the details most people overlook.

NOTES

CHAPTER 2

EXCELLENCE IS FOUND IN THE DETAILS

The smallest signals speak the loudest –
and the sharpest leaders never miss them.

STRATEGIC INSIGHT

Details don't just matter. They determine who wins the client, who earns the referral, who retains loyalty and who becomes unforgettable in a sea of competition. Many businesses operate in broad strokes. They fix the obvious and polish what's visible. But the brands that dominate, the brands that last, master the invisible layers: the subtle, repeatable, barely noticeable touches that make people say, "Something about this just feels different."

Success isn't about luck. It's about design, detail and discipline, all executed quietly in the background.

THE MOMENT IT HIT ME: BRAND LIVES IN THE INVISIBLE

Years ago, I was reviewing a proposal we were about to send to a major client. The content was solid, the pricing competitive and the strategy sharp. But something didn't feel right. Then I realised that the logo was misaligned by about two millimetres.

The font weight on the section headers was inconsistent, and one bullet point was off brand.

No one else had picked it up, but I did. Because I knew that if the presentation lacked precision, the client would assume our service did too. So, we fixed it. We aligned the grids, sharpened the spacing and cleaned the tone. The final version did not just look better but also *felt* right.

When the client finally replied, they didn't mention the pricing or strategy. They said, "This is the most professional-looking document we have ever seen."

That was the moment it clicked: brand is not just what you say. It's what people feel in the smallest, subtlest, most invisible moments. If you don't manage the invisible, you cannot expect to be seen as exceptional.

Small is not insignificant. Details accumulate, and when they do, they inspire loyalty that lasts, trust that spreads and a kind of emotional resonance that marketing cannot buy.

The best part is that it cannot be copied. Your obsession with detail becomes your competitive advantage. When looking at a proposal, a campaign or a product, most people don't even realise why they feel the way they do. They just do. That is your edge, but it's also yours to lose.

To keep the edge sharp, I ask myself and my teams: Where are the details letting us down? What is the micro that is breaking the macro? If I walked into this business for the first time today, what would I feel?

Details don't just set the tone. They *are* the tone. And that tone is your reputation.

🧠 MINDSET PRINCIPLE: THE INVISIBLE ADVANTAGE

Excellence isn't loud. It's layered, and it lives in:

- The spacing of your layout
- The cadence of your follow-up
- The posture of your team when no one's watching
- The unseen choices that silently signal: "We're intentional"

People won't always see what you did to get there, but they will feel the standard behind it.

⚠️ WARNING SIGN: WHEN THE MICRO BREAKS THE MACRO

The danger isn't just in what you miss but also in what that oversight communicates.

If you ignore the 1%, you are basically telling your team, your customers and the market: "This is acceptable." And once that signal is sent, that's when standards erode.

I've walked into billion-rand companies with broken bathroom tiles, faded brochures and disengaged front-desk staff. These aren't minor flaws. They're something I like to call "trust leaks", subtle signals that say, "We've stopped caring."

A brand doesn't fail immediately. It fades quietly, and then it suddenly collapses all at once.

💬 WHAT I TELL MY TEAMS

- "The invisible is what makes it unforgettable."
- "Precision creates presence."
- "If you don't see it, your client still feels it."
- "Details aren't cosmetic. They're strategic."

✍️ FIELD NOTES

- Excellence isn't loud; it's layered.
- People won't always notice the micro, but they'll feel the magic.
- What others overlook is where your reputation grows.
- Precision in the invisible creates trust in the visible.
- The 1% everyone ignores is what the best obsess over.

🔍 BEHIND THE CHAPTER

This chapter was born out of a near-miss I mentioned earlier, when we almost sent that proposal to the major broker we'd been trying to win for over a year.

The small details I picked up would have slipped past most people, but not me – because I know how these micro-moments shape excellence.

That's what this chapter is really about – not details for detail's sake, but the energy and trust they communicate. It's rooted in the **Execution** pillar of The Standard System™. Because in business, the invisible isn't minor; it's where your reputation is either reinforced or unravelled – one small, unspoken signal at a time.

RAISE THE STANDARD

- What detail in your brand experience have you overlooked because it felt "small"?
- What moment – visual, tonal or sensory – might be quietly eroding trust?
- If your top client walked through the doors of your business today, what would they feel?
- What invisible refinement can you make this week to turn ordinary into exceptional?

Next, we look at the power of execution and why starting means nothing if you don't finish what you commit to.

NOTES

CHAPTER 3

FINISH WHAT YOU START

Starting is easy. Finishing is everything.

STRATEGIC INSIGHT

Starting is exciting. It gives momentum, attracts applause and creates the illusion of progress. But memorable people – and businesses – are not the ones who start but those who finish. They lead companies, build legacies and transform industries because they close the loop.

Execution doesn't live in brainstorming. It lives in follow-through. You won't be remembered for what you almost did but for what you completed. Every time you finish something, even if it's tiny, you reinforce a powerful truth: I am someone who follows through.

Finishing builds trust in your team, in your clients and in yourself. But unfinished work does more than delay progress – it also corrodes belief. Eventually, people stop trusting your word, and so do you.

THE MOMENT IT HIT ME: COMMIT TO LESS, FINISH MORE

I have been involved in a number of projects where I've had this lightbulb moment: to build a culture of completion, one must commit to less but finish more.

Nowadays, I don't chase every idea. I only commit to what I know we will complete at an exceptional standard. We clearly define what "done" looks like. There are no vague updates.

We say: this is what finished looks like, and this is the time frame when it will be done. We track outcomes, not activity. We close loops in every meeting, in every handover and every decision. And we audit the graveyard. Every 90 days, we review what is "almost done". Then we either assign it, kill it or close it, so that there's no drag, dead weight or silent erosion.

MINDSET PRINCIPLE: FINISHING BUILDS IDENTITY

Every time you finish something, you prove who you are to your team, your clients and yourself. But every time you leave something incomplete, you risk fracturing that trust with half-built campaigns, half-trained teams and half-executed strategies.

These things don't just create drag; they also redefine you. Eventually, you're not seen as the visionary but as the person – or company – who doesn't close.

🛠 FRAMEWORK/PLAYBOOK: HOW I BUILD A CULTURE OF COMPLETION

Commit to Less. Finish More.
We don't chase every idea. We commit only to what we'll complete at a world-class standard.

Define "Done" Before You Start.
There are no vague "in progress" updates. We define "done", assign ownership and track it.

Track Outcomes, Not Activity.
Effort doesn't move the business. Outcomes do.

Close Every Loop.
In every meeting, we ask: *Who owns this? When will it be completed?*

Audit the Graveyard.
Every 90 days, we review the "almosts". We finish them, kill them or move on. But we do not let "half-dones" or "maybes" linger.

⚠ WARNING SIGN: THE COST OF UNFINISHED WORK

Unfinished work looks harmless – until it multiplies. During that "paused content strategy", your competitor has probably already hurtled ahead and claimed more market share. During that stalled system implementation, your team is probably improvising and dropping standards.

When it comes to just about any unassigned task, the momentum is probably gone, along with the trust.

Incompleteness isn't a delay. It's a silent drag on everything.

💬 WHAT I TELL MY TEAMS

- "Half-built work leads to half-built trust."
- "We don't get paid for motion. We get paid for outcomes."
- "Start less. Finish more."
- "If it doesn't get finished, it doesn't exist."

✍ FIELD NOTES

- Starting gets applause. Finishing earns trust.
- Completion isn't about perfection. It's about integrity.
- Open loops cost energy and belief.
- Execution lives in closure.
- Legacy isn't built on vision. It's built on delivery.

🔍 BEHIND THE CHAPTER

My father was a talented carpenter and shopfitter. But when it came to our home, projects were often left unfinished. Cupboards were built with no doors. The wine cellar was never completed. He had the skill but sometimes lacked the energy to see it through. Then he was diagnosed with multiple sclerosis when I was ten. By the time I was sixteen, he was confined to a wheelchair.

That's when I started finishing what he could not. I fixed the cupboard doors myself. I needed a sense of seeing something through to the end. That's probably where my drive to finish things comes from: a house filled with half-finished projects taught me that while starting might come easy, it's completion that gives something value.

This chapter came out of a hard lesson. We were midway through a major product rollout that had the potential to transform our commercial portfolio. But somewhere along the way, the energy faded. Ownership blurred. The loop stayed open.

One morning, I looked at our internal tracker. The product was 90% done but going nowhere. No one was blocking it, but no one was closing it either. That moment hit me hard – not because we lacked talent, but because we'd let momentum leak into ambiguity. That day, I made a rule: **"Nothing ends half-baked. Not under my name."** Because once you allow one thing to stay unfinished, you give everyone permission to do the same. Unfinished work becomes a cultural virus. It creates drift and drag and – worst of all – it kills belief.

This chapter is all about eliminating that drift. Because vision is powerful, but only if it moves and ships.

RAISE THE STANDARD

- What unfinished project is quietly weighing down your momentum?
- Where in your life or business are loops open and trust eroding because of it?
- What is one crucial thing you will finish this week?
- If your leadership was judged solely on completion, what would change?

In the next chapter, we explore how rhythm, structure and repeatability build systems that drive growth.

NOTES

CHAPTER 4

BUILD SYSTEMS THAT IMPROVE THEMSELVES

Before you build systems around you, you have to stop being the system.

STRATEGIC INSIGHT

Most entrepreneurs hit a ceiling not because they lack ambition but because they refuse to let go. The hustle that once helped them survive becomes the very thing that stops them from scaling. They pride themselves on being involved in everything – approving every quote, checking every detail and making every call. At first, it feels productive. Over time, it becomes a trap.

If your business still depends on you for everything, you haven't built a company. You've built a bottleneck – and that bottleneck is you.

THE MOMENT IT HIT ME: I REALISED I WAS THE BOTTLENECK

In 2015, I took what should have been a simple family holiday – just two weeks in Austria. Within 48 hours, my phone exploded. Approvals stalled. Clients were left waiting. My staff were frozen.

It dawned on me that everyone needed me, but nothing could move without me. I hadn't built a business; I'd built a machine that ran only when I was watching. I wasn't leading. I was holding the business together with duct tape and control.

On that supposed holiday, I realised that if the business couldn't breathe without me, I hadn't built a business; I had built a prison from which I couldn't escape.

That's when I knew: **If I'm the system, we're in trouble.**

MINDSET PRINCIPLE: THE SHIFT THAT CHANGED EVERYTHING

Letting go wasn't easy. I kind of liked being needed. It gave me control, comfort and a false sense of security. But then I started asking more powerful questions. Could someone else do this? Can this process be repeated without me? Am I creating solutions or feeding dependency?

I began to replace hustle with clarity. I shifted from asking "How fast can I do this?" to "How can we do this better without me?" I started handing off ownership – slowly, purposefully, reluctantly at first. But I did it.

The shift in mindset didn't just change my calendar and my diary; it changed the entire business culture. My teams stopped waiting for direction. They started building, fixing and leading. That's when I knew we were becoming a real company.

🛠 FRAMEWORK/PLAYBOOK: HOW I BUILD SYSTEMS THAT IMPROVE THEMSELVES

Start With the Outcome.

Every system starts by answering one question: *What must this deliver, every time and without fail?*

Diagram the Process Visually.

We record inputs, roles, tools and timelines. If it can't be mapped, it can't be scaled.

Assign Ownership, Not Just Tasks.

Every system has one name on it – not a team but the name of a person. Shared accountability is no accountability.

Automate or Template Anything That Repeats.

If it repeats, we systemise – for scale:

- Client replies
- Onboarding flows
- Performance reviews
- Department handovers

Review Every 90 Days.

We walk the system and ask:

- Is this still working?
- What's being bypassed?
- What can we simplify or improve?
- If it's not evolving, it's decaying.

⚠ WARNING SIGN: THE HIDDEN COST OF BEING THE SYSTEM

If your absence creates panic, your presence might be the problem. When everything flows through you:

- Decisions slow down
- Growth caps out
- Trust stalls
- People stay small because they're trained to be dependent

What you think is control is often just chaos in disguise.

💬 WHAT I TELL FOUNDERS

- "If you're the only one who knows how it works, it doesn't work."
- "You don't scale by doing more. You scale by becoming less essential."
- "Let go of control. Replace it with clarity."
- "If the system breaks when you step away, it was never a system. It was a habit."

✍ FIELD NOTES

- Hustle builds pressure. Systems build peace.
- If you're the system, you're also the ceiling.
- The best leaders remove themselves without the business missing a beat.
- Systems aren't just structure; they're strategy.
- Don't just solve the problem. Also solve how the problem gets solved.

BEHIND THE CHAPTER

This chapter was born on an icy mountain. I was in Austria, watching my young children ski down perfect white slopes, but I wasn't present. I was on the phone. Again. Solving things I shouldn't have had to solve. Every call, every ping and every escalation felt like a quiet confession: "You haven't built this business properly."

That's when I realised that being at the centre of everything didn't make me a great leader. It made me a liability. It hit me hard – not because the team was failing, but because I had trained them to depend on me.

For the first time, I wasn't proud of how much I was doing. I was ashamed that I had to do it all: I wasn't empowering people; I was controlling them. That shame turned into clarity, which became the new seed of delegation, structure and real leadership.

That ski trip didn't just recharge me. It rewired me. I came back and began removing myself, intentionally and permanently, from processes that didn't require my input. I began to build systems that didn't just operate but also evolved. And in doing so, I created space to lead again.

This chapter marks a critical component of The Standard System™: **Self-Awareness**. Because, before you build systems that improve themselves, you must confront that part of you that's trying to control everything and is afraid of letting go.

📝 RAISE THE STANDARD

- Where in your business are you still playing the hero instead of building the system?
- What task or process still runs only because of you?
- What could be documented, delegated or automated this week?
- What system needs a name next to it and a review on the calendar?

In the next chapter, we explore how chasing progress instead of perfection gives your team permission to move faster, think clearer and build momentum without hesitation.

NOTES

CHAPTER 5

PROGRESS OVER PERFECTION

You don't need perfect. You need movement.

STRATEGIC INSIGHT

Perfection feels noble. It tells you to wait until the timing is right, the idea is polished or every possible risk is covered. But it is often just fear in disguise – fear of being seen before your idea or product is ready, fear of judgment or fear of falling short. And while you're waiting, momentum quietly dies.

I've seen it too often: brilliant founders who never launch, teams that over-refine until the spark is gone and leaders who hesitate while the opportunity moves on. They don't fail because they made the wrong move; they fail because they made none at all.

This chapter isn't about lowering the standard. It's about knowing when to move. Some moments demand 100% momentum, but many only need 80% and the courage to sharpen in public.

The best leaders know when to polish and when to push. They don't build perfection. They build in public. Because in the real world, progress is earned by those who act, not by those who wait.

🔥 THE MOMENT IT HIT ME: HOW I LEARNED TO LET GO OF PERFECT

When we launched my high-end health and fitness business, the vision was world class. There were luxury finishes, club-style lighting, spa-grade facilities and elevated retail. It was designed to be flawless. But on launch day, the software had glitches, the team wasn't fully trained and some branded items had not arrived on time. We launched anyway.

In that first week, we learned more than we would have if we'd waited and done another six months of overplanning. We got live feedback. We fixed what mattered. We trained in real time. We adapted in motion. And within 90 days, we were no longer chasing elusive perfection; we had built something exceptional because we moved it forward.

🧠 MINDSET PRINCIPLE: WHY PROGRESS BEATS PERFECTION EVERY TIME

Perfection creates:

- Delay
- Paralysis
- Doubt
- Frustration
- Missed opportunity

Progress creates:

- Confidence
- Feedback
- Evidence
- Momentum
- Wins

Perfection is overprotective. Progress is *productive*. The one gives you a feeling of control; the other gives you impact.

FRAMEWORK/PLAYBOOK: THE ANTI-STALL FRAMEWORK

Over the years, I've developed tools to keep momentum moving. We launch fast, then we refine. We obsess over the first win – the MVP (minimum viable product) outcome that proves we are onto something. We build real-time feedback loops from day one: surveys, debriefs, observation notes and voice-of-customer tracking.

We prioritise learning, overlooking perfect or clever. Progress is driven by curiosity. And we always share the evolution. Version 1.0 is not hidden; it's shared, owned and improved on – in the open. That's when people feel included instead of left behind.

This mindset shows up across all my businesses. All new products launch in phases. Phase one is clean, functional and fast to market. Phases two and three evolve from real usage.

WARNING SIGN: WHAT HAPPENS WHEN YOU WAIT

Waiting feels safe, but the cost is brutal because:

- You miss the moment
- You lose market trust
- Your team stops believing in the momentum
- Culture starts to stall
- Confidence erodes quietly

Every time you delay in order to "perfect" something, someone else is already learning by doing it.

💬 WHAT I TELL MY TEAMS

- “Ship it. Learn. Sharpen.”
- “Done beats perfect, every time.”
- “Momentum builds trust. Waiting erodes it.”
- “If we’re stuck, we’re not leading.”
- “Launch fast. Iterate loud. Win early.”

✍ FIELD NOTES

- Waiting for perfect is just fear dressed up in a business suit.
- No one leads from the sidelines.
- Culture doesn’t reward caution. It follows motion.
- Refinement happens faster when the product is alive, not when it’s still in your head.

🔍 BEHIND THE CHAPTER

In 2019, I needed new headquarters to house my expanding business. I found the ideal space on Nicol Road in Bedfordview. Although the plans were approved, I was not financially ready for an 11-storey development – but we started anyway.

As construction unfolded, I made major changes, even while the slabs were being cast. I realised we needed another parking level. I reworked the gym layout after I woke up with a vision from a dream I’d had. Then I paused all building activity to redesign for double volume.

We went public with the gym before it was perfect. But it was better to open, get people in and evolve than to sit and polish endlessly. The restaurant followed the same path. It began as a staff canteen and evolved in full view of our customers into a world-class rooftop dining experience.

This chapter reflects another important component of The Standard System™: **Progress**. Because momentum beats perfection every time.

This way of operating is a challenge to the perfectionist in you – the part that hides behind polish to avoid the messiness and reality of creativity. I'm telling you that you don't need to be perfect. You just need to be visible and *in motion*.

📝 RAISE THE STANDARD

- What idea, offer or project have you delayed in the name of perfection?
- What's one thing you could launch at 80% this week and refine later?
- Where is ego driving delay when curiosity could drive action?
- What's one uncomfortable but courageous move you're ready to make now?

Next up, we'll explore the standards that govern how teams speak, lead and move together, because progress without alignment doesn't scale. It fractures.

NOTES

CHAPTER 6

THE RULES OF ENGAGEMENT

The way we communicate is the way we build.

STRATEGIC INSIGHT

Over the years, I've watched companies fall apart not because of poor strategies but because of how team members spoke to each other. They failed not because they lacked intelligence, but because they lacked standards for communication. There were passive-aggressive emails, gossip behind closed doors, conflict avoidance, blame deflection and vague, polite or condescending feedback. In my experience, you don't lose execution first. You lose engagement. And once engagement erodes, performance follows quickly. That's why I don't let communication evolve "organically" or leave it to chance. I engineer it with rules that hold the line before the culture slips.

THE MOMENT IT HIT ME: WHY I CREATED THESE RULES

In the early days of the business, I hired talented people who couldn't collaborate. They were brilliant at their jobs but terrible at working with each other. As a result, deadlines slipped, ideas got buried and tensions grew. But no one spoke up.

On paper, the work was solid, but inside the business, the energy was "off". People tiptoed around each other. Some checked out and trust eroded.

So, I created the first version of our Rules of Engagement: not soft values or generic slogans but clear, simple behavioural standards for how we spoke to each other, solved problems and moved together as a team. Because, in my experience, high performance requires high-trust communication. And trust isn't a feeling – it's a habit, built through tone, timing and speaking the truth.

🛠 FRAMEWORK/PLAYBOOK: THE 10 RULES OF ENGAGEMENT

Attack the Problem, Not the Person.

People often complain that conflict stresses them out. It's one thing when it's directed at a person, but when it's directed at solving a real product or customer issue, that's another story. Workplace conflict is beneficial, as long as it isn't personal.

Don't Lose Your Cool, You'll Look Like a Fool.

Losing your temper is a sign of emotional immaturity. Stats have shown that IQ drops by as much as 70% when people lose their temper. Yes, you become stupid! Emotion clouds execution. Stay composed, even under pressure.

Don't Gossip or Spread Rumours About Your Co-Workers.

Talking badly about a colleague when they aren't there to defend themselves, says more about you than them. If you don't know the whole story, don't tell any of it. If you can't say it directly, don't say it at all.

Instead of Making Waves, Make Decisions.
Dysfunctional employees love to disrupt things and create turmoil. Instead of making waves – dive in, analyse the problem and propose a solution.

Tell It Straight, Don't Sugar-Coat.
That's right. Grow some balls! Be honest about what's going on, and accept nothing less from others. Being a "yes" person or surrounding yourself with other "yes" people spells disaster for you and your organisation.

Instead of Covering Your Ass, Put Your Ass on the Line.
Nobody has ever advanced in their career by covering their ass and nobody has ever gotten ahead without taking risks. No pain, no gain. Simple as that.

To Break Analysis Paralysis, Take a Chill Pill.
A few chronic debaters can effectively stall all decision-making. Entire organisations can come to a grinding halt. Instead of flogging a dead horse, chill out, then meet back and document a decision. You can always change it later, but not if you don't make the call.

Instead of Protecting Your Turf, Open Up the Playing Field.
The more you try to protect your domain, the faster you'll lose it. Turf wars quickly deteriorate into dysfunctional silo behaviour and bunker mentality. It's all bad for business. There's enough space for everyone to win.

Don't Blame, Take Responsibility.

Pointing fingers at your colleagues just creates tension or inflames already tense situations. By identifying and taking responsibility for issues, you bring them to light and resolve them quicker, and you'll be recognised for your effort.

Acknowledge the Problem.

Share your feelings. A grudge can develop when an issue isn't fully confronted. To get a better understanding of the other person, try putting yourself in their shoes.

Accept what is. Choose to create your own closure with or without an apology. Don't dwell on it. Once you've decided to move on, keep on moving. Take away the positive lessons. Let it go. This allows room for peace and happiness. Forgive. No one is perfect, and we all make mistakes.

⚠ WARNING SIGN: WHAT HAPPENS WHEN YOU DON'T DEFINE THE RULES

If your team doesn't know how to:

- Raise issues
- Disagree with leadership
- Handle tension
- Deliver feedback
- Speak hard truths

Then culture collapses in silence – not with shouting, but through avoidance, hesitation and disengagement. Trust dies quietly. Engagement turns to politeness. Energy wanes, and long before the resignation letters arrive, people check out emotionally.

🗩 WHAT I TELL MY TEAMS

- "High performance needs high trust."
- "Don't speak around it; speak to it."
- "Tone is culture. Silence is culture. Everything we do is culture."
- "This is how we move. This is how we protect the brand."

✍ FIELD NOTES

- Execution breaks when communication drifts.
- Culture lives in tone, timing and truth.
- If the energy is off, start by fixing how people speak to each other.
- Teams don't need agreement; they need alignment.
- Trust is built on how we handle tension, not on how we avoid it.

🔍 BEHIND THE CHAPTER

This chapter came out of a collision I didn't see coming. I wrote it after two of my top performers clashed but no one addressed it. There was boardroom diplomacy, with polite faces and passive tension – everyone felt it, but no one dealt with it. Deadlines slipped. Energy dropped. Trust was eroded throughout the team.

When I called the two warring parties in, they admitted they didn't know how to have the hard conversation – not because they didn't care, but because they didn't know how to engage cleanly without conflict. That's when I realised: communication isn't personality-driven. It's standard-driven.

If you don't give people a framework dealing with tension, they'll avoid it, and drift becomes the culture.

We no longer leave communication up to chance or emotion. We build it into how we work. Because the way we talk to each other is how we lead and succeed.

📝 RAISE THE STANDARD

- Where in your business is silence replacing truth?
- What conversations aren't happening, and at what cost?
- Which of these 10 rules do your team need to rehearse, not just remember?
- What would change if tone became as important as tasks?

Now, let's recap what you've learned in Part 1.

NOTES

🔁 PART I RECAP – MINDSET: THE INTERNAL STANDARD

Before you scale a business, you build the standard inside yourself.

Your business is only as strong as the standards you set. This section wasn't about gimmicks or hype; it was about identity. Because systems don't scale if the people building them drift off course.

Before you build brands, teams or products, you build yourself. The previous six chapters form the foundation of The Standard System™, your internal operating code for building something exceptional from the inside out.

📌 WHAT YOU'VE JUST MASTERED

Chapter 1: Strive for Perfection, Knowing You'll Never Achieve It

The pursuit of perfection isn't about flawlessness. It's about refusing to tolerate the average – and then using precision as a daily standard.

Chapter 2: Excellence is Found in the Details

Details are never cosmetic. They're strategic. What's invisible to most is what defines how your brand is remembered.

Chapter 3: Finish What You Start

Execution is identity. Every unclosed loop weakens momentum. Completion is the leadership trait that earns trust and defines culture.

Chapter 4: Build Systems That Improve Themselves

Freedom comes when you stop being the system and start designing one. Leadership isn't about presence; it's about architecture.

Chapter 5: Progress Over Perfection

Waiting for "perfect" is just fear in disguise. Movement beats mastery. Leaders don't delay; they build while refining.

Chapter 6: The Rules of Engagement

Culture begins with communication. How your team members talk to each other is how your brand moves. Tone is not personal; it's operational.

YOUR SELF-AUDIT: SIX QUESTIONS TO REFLECT ON

1. What am I still tolerating about myself that I'd never accept from my team?
2. What detail am I overlooking that might be breaking trust quietly?
3. What's currently stuck at 80% and needs to be finished this week?
4. Where am I still the bottleneck? What system needs to replace me?
5. What idea or strategy have I delayed in the name of perfection?
6. What unspoken communication rule is silently shaping our culture?

THE SHIFT

Great businesses are built on standards, not on pie-in-the-sky dreams or unattainable goals. You don't scale through motivation but through mindset. Mindset is a habit – the decisions you repeat when the pressure is on, and the tone you protect before strategy, before brand and before launch.

Part I has given you the mindset foundation to lead with clarity, consistency and conviction, regardless of the pressure, mood or motivation in the room. Take just one idea from this section and apply it this week. Raise the bar in a visible, undeniable way. Because when your internal standard sharpens, everything around you starts to shift.

In the next chapter, we move from tone to teams. We explore how care, ownership and culture shape a company that people want to build from the inside out.

NOTES

PART II

STRUCTURE: BUILD WHAT LASTS

CHAPTER 7

FROM CULTURE TO REPUTATION

Your brand isn't what you say; it's what people feel when you're not in the room, because what people feel is what they remember.

STRATEGIC INSIGHT

Over the years, I've come to believe that culture is the soil and reputation is the fruit. You can spend millions on branding, logos, websites, campaigns and strategy decks, but if the experience doesn't match the promise, you've already lost your audience.

People might not read your pitch, but they feel your presence. They might not quote your slogan, but they repeat your name, either with admiration or with caution and derision. Your brand isn't built by what you post on social media. It's built by what your team consistently protects, when no one is watching.

This chapter reflects the **Culture** pillar of The Standard System™, because if the internal environment is inconsistent, unclear or misaligned, the market will feel it before you say a word.

🔥 THE MOMENT IT HIT ME: REPUTATION WAS ALREADY SPEAKING FOR ME

A year or so ago, I walked into a boardroom to meet a major broker group. Before I said a word, one of the principals leaned across the table and said: “We’ve heard about you. You don’t miss deadlines. You don’t delay feedback. You don’t tolerate excuses.”

That had nothing to do with marketing. He’d never met me, but he’d encountered the standard we had set in the market. It wasn’t our website that impressed him. It was our culture, delivery and follow-through.

That’s when it clicked: **the standard you protect on the inside is what becomes your reputation on the outside.**

🧠 MINDSET PRINCIPLE: WHAT REPUTATION IS ACTUALLY BUILT ON

Reputation isn’t your design system. It’s your operating system, reflected back to you by the market. It’s the compound result of:

- The way your team works under pressure
- The tone of your communication when things go wrong
- The speed of your follow-up
- The way the business *feels,* even in quiet moments
- The consistency between what you say and what you deliver

You can’t fake it. You can’t outsource it. It’s not what you market; it’s what you maintain.

🛠 FRAMEWORK/PLAYBOOK: HOW I PROTECT THE CULTURE THAT BUILDS REPUTATION

We Hire for Alignment, Not Just Talent.
Skill gets you noticed. Alignment makes you credible. We hire people who *protect the brand* instead of just "doing the job".

We Train for Reputation-Building Moments.
The real test isn't when everything is running smoothly. It's when things go sideways. We train for the pressure, because that's where our brand either improves or collapses.

We Fix the Feeling, Not Just the Issue.
Solving the problem is step one, but rebuilding trust means resolving how the client felt during the failure.

We Say Less. We Deliver More.
We don't hype or oversell. We create systems that speak for themselves.

We Own Mistakes Early and Fix Them Publicly.
Reputation isn't built on perfection. It's built on how fast you say, "That's on us. Here's what we're doing about it."

⚠ WARNING SIGN: THE COST OF CULTURE DRIFT

If your culture stops caring, your reputation starts decaying. If your values are only on the wall, your delivery becomes inconsistent. And if you say you're premium but your team shows up tired, late or vague, you're not a premium brand – you're a scripted brand. The market knows the difference and won't believe what you say. Your clients will believe how you make them feel.

💬 WHAT I TELL MY TEAMS

- “Our reputation starts where the pitch ends.”
- “Every behaviour is a brand message.”
- “Clients don’t remember what we say. They remember how we make them feel.”
- “If it’s not consistent inside, it’s already broken outside.”
- “Protect the promise, even when it’s inconvenient.”

✍ FIELD NOTES

- Culture is the internal brand. Reputation is the external result.
- What your team does daily becomes what the market repeats.
- Precision on the inside becomes credibility on the outside.
- Reputation doesn’t start in marketing; it starts in meetings.
- People feel your brand long before they engage with your product.

🔍 BEHIND THE CHAPTER

This chapter was born in a moment of clarity and pride. When that broker said, “We’ve heard about you,” I felt something deeper than validation. I felt *alignment*, because it’s one thing to land a pitch but another thing entirely when your **culture precedes you**.

It reminded me that reputation isn’t what you say when people are watching. It’s what the world whispers when you’re not in the room. That whisper is built on:

- The way your team answers the phone when no one’s listening
- The way a proposal lands when no one asks for polish
- The tone of your decline when you walk away from the wrong client

Reputation is the echo of your culture. Once you realise that, you'll stop branding from the outside in and start building from the inside out.

RAISE THE STANDARD

- What internal habits are shaping your reputation without you realising it?
- What do clients feel *before* you speak, and what does that say about your culture?
- What's one behaviour you need to amend this week to protect the promise of your brand?
- What would happen if your brand stopped trying to impress and started staying consistent?

In the following chapter, we move from setting the standard to sharing the weight, and we explore how real leadership creates a culture where accountability is lived, not forced.

NOTES

CHAPTER 8

CREATING A CULTURE OF ACCOUNTABILITY

If no one owns it, nothing moves.

STRATEGIC INSIGHT

Accountability is not about pressure, control or catching people out. It's about **ownership** and creating a culture where every person knows:

- What they're responsible for
- What success looks like
- When a project or product is due
- What happens when it doesn't happen

Without this clarity, you don't have alignment. You have busyness. And busy teams don't scale – they stall.

THE MOMENT IT HIT ME: ACCOUNTABILITY WAS THE MISSING LINK

Years ago, we hit a wave of growth. There were more clients, products and staff, yet performance slowed down, deadlines slipped and projects stalled. Updates floated around inboxes for weeks. Everyone was "working on it", but no one was finishing it.

That's when I looked at the organisational chart and asked, "Who actually owns this?" The answer: "No one." We had great people but unclear lines. We had involvement but lacked ownership. So, I made a rule: Everything gets a name next to it. Not a team. Not a department. A person.

It changed everything.

🧠 MINDSET PRINCIPLE: WHAT ACCOUNTABILITY REALLY CREATES

- Speed
- Trust
- Clarity
- Confidence
- Cultural strength

Because when people own the outcome, momentum grows. When no one owns it, everything starts to drift.

🛠️ FRAMEWORK/PLAYBOOK: HOW I BUILD A CULTURE OF OWNERSHIP

Name the Owner.

Every initiative has one name next to it. Not a group. Not a role. A name. If it fails, we don't wonder who's responsible – we know.

Make Tracking Public.

Everyone sees what's on track, slipping or overdue. Sunlight speeds up progress.

Call It Early.

If something is drifting, we don't wait. We raise it – fast, clear, and with respect. Accountability delayed becomes underperformance normalised.

Use Outcome-Based Language.

We don't ask, "Are you working on it?" We ask, "Is it done?" Effort is appreciated. Completion is required.

Model It From the Top.

If I miss something, I own up first. If I drop the ball, I call it myself. I've learned that when leaders deflect, everyone else learns to disappear and not take ownership.

⚠ WARNING SIGN: THE COST OF VAGUE RESPONSIBILITY

Many leaders confuse accountability with pressure, clarity with micromanagement, and ownership with blame. But true accountability is empowerment. It says: "You matter so much to the mission that we are giving you a name, a deadline and a lane to run in."

When accountability fades, so does energy. People start saying:

- "I assumed they were handling it."
- "I thought we were still waiting."
- "I wasn't sure who was leading."

It's not miscommunication; it's a **leadership vacuum**. Without clear ownership, deadlines become mere guidelines and performance becomes optional.

WHAT I TELL MY TEAMS

- "You don't get in trouble for mistakes. You get in trouble for hiding them."
- "If you see the problem, it's yours until it's solved or escalated."
- "Ownership isn't pressure; it's power."
- "If everyone's responsible, no one is."

FIELD NOTES

- A task without an owner is a risk waiting to happen.
- Culture isn't what people say; it's what they own.
- Clarity kills drift.
- Deadlines aren't scary when you're trusted to deliver.
- Accountability turns motion into momentum.

BEHIND THE CHAPTER

This chapter came to me after a breakdown in execution. A respected industry publication offered us a monthly feature article. Everyone was excited.

The first article was submitted on time. The second barely made it. By the time the deadline for the third arrived, no one knew who was writing it. Needless to say, the whole initiative collapsed.

After digging deeper, I realised no one had actually taken responsibility. There was no twelve-month plan, no clear leader and no real accountability. The ball was dropped because no one was holding it. That's when I banned the phrase "We're all responsible". Because that is how things slip through the cracks while everyone swears that they care.

Culture doesn't thrive on collaboration alone. It needs clear ownership, too. And when ownership is embedded, the atmosphere changes. People move with intention, speak with clarity and show up knowing their contribution matters.

This chapter reflects a vital principle of The Standard System™: **Ownership**. Because until someone owns it, nothing will happen.

RAISE THE STANDARD

- What initiative in your business is drifting because no one owns it?
- Where are you tolerating group ownership when it really needs a single name?
- What's one outcome this week that needs a clear owner and a visible deadline?
- How are you modelling accountability – loudly, publicly and without excuses?

In the next chapter, we explore how vision, when divorced from ego, becomes your clearest and most powerful leadership tool.

NOTES

CHAPTER 9

LEADING WITH VISION, NOT EGO

If your leadership is about you, your business stops with you.

STRATEGIC INSIGHT

The biggest threat in business is not the market. It's not inflation, competition or global shifts either. It's ego in leadership. Toxic ego builds empires that implode. It creates teams that obey but don't believe. It slows decision-making, breeds resentment and turns leaders into obstacles. Ego makes everything about you, and when you are at the centre of everything, nothing moves without you.

But when you lead with vision instead of ego and with humility instead of arrogance, everything changes. You multiply loyalty. You scale trust. You build something that doesn't die when you step away. Because ego needs you, while vision survives you.

THE MOMENT IT HIT ME: MY OWN STRUGGLE WITH CONTROL

In the early years, I wanted to be in charge of everything – not because I didn't trust my team, but because I believed my way was the only way. I had built the business from scratch, and I believed I was the only one who truly understood it.

Every campaign needed my sign-off. Every new hire passed through me. Every process required my approval. It felt like leadership, but it was actually control. Eventually, I realised: I'm not building a business; I'm building a bottleneck.

We had hit something that I call the "S-curve". It's a well-known concept in business that refers to the moment when the old way no longer works because it won't take the business to the next level. Many leaders and entrepreneurs get stuck in this comfort zone. They cling to control and become the constraint.

My success has come from recognising these S-curves and making changes ahead of the curve, because leadership means knowing when to evolve and when to get out of your own way.

The first S-curve I hit in the business was a game changer. I realised that without drastic change, the business would stagnate. And the truth was clear: it couldn't grow if I remained at the centre of everything.

So, I let go. It was difficult. Control had been my comfort zone, but it had also become my ceiling. Once I stepped back, we scaled. That was the moment I became a real leader. And it's why my businesses thrive today, because they no longer rely totally on me.

🧠 MINDSET PRINCIPLE: WHAT VISION-LED LEADERSHIP LOOKS LIKE

Build Systems, Not Dependence.
Ego wants to be the hero. Vision builds the machine that helps to create the blueprint and empowers others to run it.

Hire People Smarter Than You.
If you're the best at everything, you're either in the wrong business or you're afraid to grow. Ego fears talent. Vision recruits it.

Share the Spotlight.
You don't need admiration and credit; you need humility. Celebrate others more loudly than you celebrate yourself.

Listen More Than You Speak.
You don't need to prove your intelligence. You create space for talent to rise, often from voices newer and younger than yours.

Own Your Mistakes Publicly.
Nothing builds trust like a leader who says, "I got it wrong. Here's how I'll fix it." Because when you display humility, your team learns to lead without fear.

⚠ WARNING SIGN: THE COST OF EGO-BASED LEADERSHIP

When everything relies on you, the business becomes rigid. You delay decisions. You create dependencies. You choke initiative. You exhaust yourself and quietly demoralise your team. And eventually, the best people leave – not because of the product, but because they're tired of waiting for permission.

💬 WHAT I TELL MY LEADERS

- "If the business falls apart when you're away, you haven't built a company; you've built a leash."
- "Your job is not to be irreplaceable. It's to multiply others."
- "Ego wants applause. Vision wants alignment."
- "You're not here to control. You're here to empower."

✍ FIELD NOTES

- Vision scales. Ego suffocates.
- The strongest leaders are the most replaceable by design.
- Letting go isn't a weakness; it's maturity.
- Your real legacy is built in systems, not in the spotlight.
- Great companies are led by founders who made space, not noise.

🔍 BEHIND THE CHAPTER

This chapter was forged in one of the hardest moments of my life. I had been hiding the severity of my opioid addiction from everyone. I had been trying to recover alone, and it wasn't working.

One day, I invited my senior management team to a meeting. Twenty-five people walked into the boardroom. They had no idea what was coming. I stood in front of them and told them the hard and ugly truth about the motorcycle accident, the painkillers, the dependency and the withdrawals. I was in tears as I opened up about the burdens I had been carrying behind the scenes.

When I finished, the room was silent, and the atmosphere was heavy. Many people were teary-eyed, and no one judged me. In fact, they respected me more for being honest. That moment, that dissolution of my ego, brought us closer together than ever. And it taught me one of the greatest leadership lessons of my life: ego separates leaders from people. Humility and honesty bring them together.

I first began confronting this truth back in Chapter 4, when I realised that I had built a bottleneck instead of a business. But in front of my exco, this was the moment of truth: I didn't just need systems, I also had to surrender, get out of my own way and lead from a humbler place.

This chapter reflects the driving force behind The Standard System™: **Vision**. Because when you lead with purpose instead of pride, your business becomes bigger than you – and stronger because of it.

RAISE THE STANDARD

- Where in your leadership are you still holding on because it makes you feel safe?
- What system, decision or process could move faster without you in the middle?
- What would change if your team saw your honesty as a strength, not a crack?
- What would leading with humility, not ego, look like for you this week?

In the next chapter, we'll explore the most avoided, and most powerful word in business, and why the leaders who use it build the kind of trust nothing else can match.

NOTES

CHAPTER 10

THE MOST POWERFUL WORD IN BUSINESS

An apology builds trust faster than strategy ever will.

STRATEGIC INSIGHT

"Sorry" is the most avoided word in business – and the most powerful. It disarms conflict, restores trust, and models the kind of courage that turns blame into clarity. Most businesses overcomplicate recovery, but in my experience, one sincere, early apology changes everything. Apologising is not a sign of weakness but one of accountability and credibility. And when paired with real ownership, it becomes the most strategic move a leader can make.

THE MOMENT IT HIT ME: WHEN I CHOSE APOLOGY OVER DEFENCE

A few years back, we avoided a catastrophic fire loss in my insurance business. The client had failed to comply with long-standing risk requirements, so we issued a formal non-renewal.

When the fire broke out, we were no longer on risk. Proud of the team's foresight, I shared the story with our brokers in a mailer. But I hadn't considered the impact on the high-profile client.

They were publicly listed, and the implication – even without actually naming them – caused reputational fallout. Their broker was furious and the client felt exposed.

When it came to my attention, I didn't defend myself. I called for a meeting and I opened it with a full, direct, no-strings-attached apology. Then I followed up with a written public apology. No spin. No legal filters. Just ownership.

That moment shifted everything. The tension drained. The conversation opened. And we left with trust intact.

🧠 MINDSET PRINCIPLE: WHY APOLOGY = OWNERSHIP

Most leaders are taught to lead from a place of confidence and control. But real trust is earned through vulnerability, not posturing. A well-timed, sincere apology is a signal that your leadership is grounded – not in ego, but in ownership. It shows you value relationships over reputation, and resolution over defence.

Great leadership isn't about always being right. It's about responding right when you've been wrong. In a world full of polished statements and strategic distancing, a leader who says "I'm sorry" – and means it – is magnetic. That level of humility is rare – and people will follow leaders who own their mistakes faster than they'll follow the perfect ones who hide behind ego.

🛠 FRAMEWORK/PLAYBOOK: THE ANATOMY OF A REAL APOLOGY

Clear Ownership

Don't just say sorry – be specific: "We failed to deliver on X", or "I dropped the ball on Y". Vague apologies mean nothing. Ownership shows courage.

No Deflection

Never hide behind process, policy or people. Even if others were involved, your job as a leader is to carry the weight. "We're sorry, but ..." is not an apology. It's a negotiation.

Visible Correction

The fastest way to rebuild trust is to fix what is broken – visibly and decisively. That means refunds, replacements, restructuring, or direct follow-throughs. Show that you mean your apology. Don't just say it.

Behavioural Consistency

Apologies lose meaning when followed by repeat offences. Your future actions must validate your words. The standard you set after the mistake you make is what people will remember – not the moment of remorse.

Speed Over Spin

Apologise early. The longer you wait, the more it looks like strategy, not sincerity. If the apology includes the word "but", it's not an apology. That's spin. And spin ruins trust.

⚠ WARNING SIGN: WHAT HAPPENS WHEN YOU DON'T OWN IT FAST ENOUGH

Most leaders and companies don't lose trust because of the mistakes they made; they lose it in how they responded.

When things go wrong, silence often feels safer. Teams craft polished statements or hide behind policy. Leaders send emails, laced with vague explanations, without admitting any wrongdoing. They make promises without changing anything, and deflect without owning up. And every one of those responses sends a message: "We care more about optics than accountability."

That's when trust begins to decay. Clients disengage. Employees stop raising concerns. Partners stop believing the brand. And by the time the reputational damage surfaces, it's often too late to fix it with words.

In an age of hyper-exposure, silence doesn't protect. It poisons. And spin doesn't save face; it accelerates mistrust. You don't rebuild trust by being careful. You rebuild it by being clear.

💬 WHAT I TELL MY TEAMS

- "Say it early. Say it fully. Say it once."
- "The fastest way to rebuild trust is with truth."
- "We don't do spin. We do ownership."
- "Sorry is not strategy. It's leadership."
- "If it needs a lawyer to sound sincere, it's not sincere."

✍ FIELD NOTES

- A real apology earns more trust than silence ever will.
- The quicker the apology, the stronger the recovery.
- Apology culture starts at the top.
- Sorry isn't a tactic. It's the tone that defines your brand.
- A visible, sincere apology fixes more than a legal letter ever will.

BEHIND THE CHAPTER

This chapter sits at the heart of how I lead. Across every business I've built, the ability to apologise – clearly, early and sincerely – has been non-negotiable. It's a key cultural principle in all my businesses, and a test of whether someone is truly ready to carry weight.

I've seen firsthand how a well-timed apology can disarm conflict, save relationships, and rebuild trust – faster than any discount, refund, or strategy ever could. And I've also seen how the lack of one – when leaders hide behind policy, delay responsibility or resort to excuses instead of taking ownership – can unravel everything. It doesn't matter how competent you are, if you can't apologise, you can't lead people. And that's why I believe that "sorry" is the most powerful word in the world of business.

RAISE THE STANDARD

- When was the last time you said sorry as a leader?
- Where in your business has deflection replaced ownership?
- What relationship in your life needs an apology, not another email?
- How could your team culture change if you modelled visible apology?
- What would happen if your standard became: "We own it first"?

In the next chapter, we explore the one skill that determines how your message lands, how your culture holds, and how your leadership is felt, even in silence. It's not a tactic – it's the emotional operating system behind everything that lasts.

NOTES

CHAPTER 11

THE EQ STANDARD

Emotional intelligence isn't soft. It's the system behind every hard decision that lands right.

STRATEGIC INSIGHT

In leadership, technical skills get you through the door and through the pitch – but emotional intelligence (EQ) is what gets you through the storm.

You can't scale with brittle leadership, or retain talent without emotional safety. And you can't protect your culture if you can't read the room. EQ isn't "nice to have". It's operational. It's the difference between a leader who reacts and a leader who reads the room. It's what separates a manager who enforces compliance from a builder who creates alignment.

There have been times when I've led without EQ. I've made decisions while emotionally shut down, and I've been defensive when I should have been listening. I've spoken when silence would have served me better, and I've felt the cost of ignoring what others were feeling. I've learnt the hard way that emotional intelligence isn't about being soft; it's about being sharp.

If strategy is how we move teams, then EQ is how we keep them together while doing it. As AI continues to replicate intelligence, our emotional intelligence is becoming our most precious human advantage; the one leadership skill that machines can't mimic.

🔥 THE MOMENT IT HIT ME: WHEN I LOST THE ROOM

A couple of years ago, I was in a boardroom, delivering what I thought was a clear, confident directive to my executive team. I was so focused on the goal, the numbers and the urgency of my speech that I hardly noticed that some members of my exco were no longer looking at me, and their energy had dropped. They weren't hearing the message; they were hearing my disconnected tone.

Later that day, one of my most trusted leaders pulled me aside and said, "You didn't hear us, Antonio. You simply steamrolled us." She was right. I hadn't asked a single question, and I hadn't read the room. I had bulldozed forward with conviction, but without any connection to the people in the meeting.

That conversation hit hard, not because I was wrong, but because I was blind to my own preoccupation. And in that moment, I realised something I had been avoiding for years: I had trained myself to operate at high intensity, but hadn't trained myself to listen emotionally. Yes, I had clarity in my strategy, but zero bandwidth for what my team was feeling. That was the day I stopped seeing EQ as optional. I started treating it like a muscle, one I needed to build if I wanted to lead at the next level.

MINDSET PRINCIPLE: FEEL IT, DON'T FEED IT

Emotional intelligence doesn't mean you suppress emotion. Rather, it means you recognise it, regulate it, and respond from a place of clarity, not chaos.

The most dangerous leaders aren't the loud ones or the emotional ones – they're the unaware ones, the ones who don't know how they're landing. They're the ones who walk into a room and change the atmosphere without realising it, or worse still, without caring. EQ is the antidote to that blindness.

It starts with self-awareness: knowing what you're feeling, where it's coming from, and how it's showing up in your behaviour. Then it moves to self-regulation: staying grounded when the room's on fire, when your ego's been bruised, or when fear tries to masquerade as decisiveness.

But the highest level of EQ is social awareness: reading what others aren't saying. It's about feeling the tension before it escalates, and sensing when your team is burnt out even though they seem to be performing. It's the ability to hold space, not just give direction.

EQ is not about being emotional. It's about being intelligent with emotion.

FRAMEWORK/PLAYBOOK: HOW I SYSTEMISE EQ INTO LEADERSHIP

I don't leave EQ to chance. I've learned to engineer it into my rhythm, just like I would with any other system. Here's how I do it across my teams and decisions:

Pause Before you Push.
Before I respond, direct or escalate – I pause. I ask: "Is this frustration, fear or fact?" That one-second gap between stimulus and response is where leadership lives.

Label the Emotion Without Letting it Lead.
I train myself and my leaders to name what they're feeling, not to dramatise it, but to disarm it.

- "I'm feeling defensive right now."
- "This feels like a breach of trust, not just a missed deadline."
- Naming emotions gives you power over them.

Audit the Atmosphere.
Every week, I scan the emotional temperature of the business:

- Who has checked out but is still delivering?
- Who are tense even when their work is solid?
- Who's disconnected after feedback?

These are early signs of cultural fracture. EQ catches them before they compound.

Hold Space Before you Solve.
Not every concern needs a solution. Sometimes, people just need to feel safe enough to speak up.

EQ is all about listening to understand, not listening to respond.

Coach Emotionally, not Just Operationally.
When giving feedback, I go deeper:

- "What was going on within you when that happened?"
- "What story were you telling yourself?"

EQ coaching transforms correction into growth.

Model Regulated Leadership.
I first regulate, and then lead. Because: Calm is contagious, and so is chaos. Presence beats performance.

Over time, I've come to realise that behind all these practices, sit five foundational traits. These are the real architecture of emotional intelligence:

- Self-awareness – recognising your emotional state
- Self-regulation – managing your responses
- Motivation – leading with internal drive, not ego
- Empathy – reading others' emotions accurately
- Social skills – navigating relationships, tension, and influence, with emotional precision

⚠ WARNING SIGN: WHEN EQ IS MISSING, TRUST SLIPS QUIETLY

Most leadership failures don't start with bad strategy. They start with emotional misfires:

- A great message delivered with a poor tone
- Staff who stop speaking because it's no longer safe
- A tense room that no one addresses
- A leadership culture that rewards performance but ignores people

When EQ is missing, trust erodes quietly. Culture softens. Energy disappears. And no one can tell you why, until it's too late.

EQ is the early warning system. Without it, you don't see the cracks until the whole thing collapses.

💬 WHAT I TELL MY TEAMS

- Check the room before you check the box.
- You're not managing a task. You're managing energy.
- EQ doesn't mean you soften. It means you connect.
- Control your tone before it controls the message.
- If you can't read the room, you can't lead the room.
- Presence isn't about being in the meeting. It's about being felt in the moment.
- You don't have to agree to understand. You just have to listen.

✍ FIELD NOTES

- Emotional intelligence is leadership under pressure.
- Strategy lands better when the tone carries trust.
- Teams don't quit jobs; they quit how it feels to be led.
- EQ turns hard conversations into growth conversations.
- Feedback without EQ becomes criticism.
- Leaders set the emotional tone, whether they mean to or not.
- You can't scale what you can't feel.
- EQ isn't soft. It's what moves people. And people move results.

The most consistent cultures are the ones that feel safe to challenge and be challenged. If your presence drains the room, your leadership isn't working.

🔍 BEHIND THE CHAPTER

This chapter was born in 2017, the year Alpha's culture cracked.

People were insecure in their jobs, but afraid to speak up. Meetings were quiet in all the wrong ways. Decisions were delayed, truthful conversations were avoided, and the air was thick with unspoken tensions. The company was growing, but beneath the surface, people were surviving me, not following me. And I knew exactly where the problem had started – with me.

A fish rots from the head. That's a truth most leaders tend to avoid. But I couldn't. I had to take a long, honest look in the mirror and admit that I had created an environment built on pressure instead of presence, and intensity instead of empathy.

People were performing to protect themselves, not because they felt empowered. I had to admit that the person who had built this culture was me. So if I didn't change, nothing else would.

That was the beginning of my journey into emotional intelligence. I didn't learn it from a book, but from pain. My awakening came from realising the uncomfortable truth that technical brilliance, without emotional awareness, is not leadership. It's a liability.

But I only truly honed EQ during my recovery from opioid addiction, which stripped away every layer of my image, identity and certainty I'd ever built. I had to learn how to feel without collapsing, how to listen without defending, and how to lead when all I wanted to do was hide.

EQ didn't make me softer. It made me sharper, stronger and more trustworthy. It made me human.

I have written this chapter because strategy may move the business forward, but EQ is what keeps it from falling apart.

RAISE THE STANDARD

- Where in your leadership are you reacting instead of reading?
- What relationship is suffering because you've been emotionally unavailable, even if unintentionally?
- Where have you prioritised performance over presence, or control over connection?
- What's one conversation this week where you could listen fully, without solving or defending?
- What would shift in your business if EQ became a standard – not a trait, but a system?

In the next chapter, we shift from leading from the front to lifting from below, and we explore how empowering the next generation is your most scalable investment.

NOTES

CHAPTER 12

EMPOWERING THE NEXT GENERATION

Legacy isn't what you leave behind. It's who you lift up.

STRATEGIC INSIGHT

There comes a moment in every leader's journey when the scoreboard stops being enough and the metrics no longer matter. You've built your business. You've proven yourself and achieved what others said was impossible – and then the deeper question dawns on you: Who am I building next? Because real legacy isn't a brand, a business or a balance sheet. It's people, and their potential. It's the human beings who rise and prosper because you created space, belief and structure for them.

Empowering others is not just a value, but also a multiplier. It's the foundation of sustainable leadership and a core aspect of The Standard System™.

THE MOMENT IT HIT ME: WHY I INVEST IN THE NEXT GENERATION

Because I *was* once the next generation. I was the 16-year-old pizza boy working late nights in a restaurant. I was twenty-something with big dreams but no clear plans. I was that kid with pressure on his shoulders and fire in his chest. I know what it feels like to have drive without support and potential without a platform.

In the early days of my business, I was the 24-year-old broker pretending I wasn't the owner, because no one trusted someone that young with multimillion-rand portfolios. So, when I see young talent today, I don't just see potential. I also see responsibility.

Because if I don't bet on them, who will?

🧠 MINDSET PRINCIPLE: WHAT EMPOWERMENT REALLY MEANS

Empowerment goes beyond giving someone a title. It's also about giving them something real to carry, prove and protect.

It means:

- Letting people lead before they feel ready
- Funding their future before they've proven anything
- Coaching them through mindsets, not just tasks
- Modelling what pressure, poise and presence actually look like

Empowerment isn't about favours or sympathy. It's strategic and it's scalable – when done with intent.

🛠 FRAMEWORK/PLAYBOOK: HOW I BUILD FUTURE LEADERS

I Hire For Hunger, Not History.

Experience matters, but hunger moves faster. I'll back the 19-year-old with drive and ambition over the veteran with ego – every time.

I Give Real Responsibility Early.

If they show initiative, they get ownership. They're given support, accountability and room to fail, but also real weight to carry.

I Fund the Version of Them They Haven't Met Yet.

I pay for development, training and certifications, not as a favour but as a long-term investment.

I Teach Frameworks; I Don't Just Give Instructions.

I don't want doers; I want builders. I explain the *why*, not just the *how*, so they can lead and not simply repeat.

I Model the Standard Daily.

I instil discipline, decision-making and intelligence. They don't learn it from my lectures but from how I show up.

⚠ WARNING SIGN: THE RISK NO ONE TALKS ABOUT

Investing in young people isn't easy. They'll make mistakes. They'll test your patience. They'll fail – sometimes spectacularly. But that's the cost of building people instead of just hiring them. And the return on investment grows exponentially, in ways money never can.

💬 WHAT I TELL YOUNG BUILDERS

- "You don't need to be ready. You need to be real."
- "Care more. Show up sharper. Own the room, then raise it."
- "Earn your seat. Protect the culture. Elevate everyone around you."
- "Leadership doesn't start with a title. It starts with how you carry yourself."

✍ FIELD NOTES

- You don't scale a company without scaling people.
- Titles don't create leaders. Trust does.
- Empowerment isn't passive; it's engineered.
- Give people something real to carry. Then support them as they learn how.
- Legacy isn't a brand. It's a young builder you've developed.

🔍 BEHIND THE CHAPTER

I wrote this chapter after watching a 25-year-old on my team challenge a senior exco member with clarity, confidence and care – not out of arrogance, but because he was aligned. He had been mentored, trusted and invested in. He was not acting like a rebel; he was acting like a leader. That moment reminded me: **The best leaders aren't those who need to be followed. They're the ones who create more leaders.**

This chapter reflects another crucial tool within The Standard System™: **Multiplication**. It means developing people who can lead others, not just by doing the work but also by growing the work through others. When leadership stops with you, so does the business.

RAISE THE STANDARD

- Who in your world has potential but no platform yet?
- What real responsibility could you trust them with this month?
- Where are you playing gatekeeper instead of mentor?
- What investment of time, trust or training could create a leader who outgrows you?

In the next chapter, we shift from nurturing potential to activating progress and exploring how to move from idea to execution without delays.

NOTES

CHAPTER 13

FROM IDEA TO EXECUTION

Ideas are cheap. Execution builds empires.

STRATEGIC INSIGHT

Everyone has ideas – the barista, the intern, even your cousin who pitches his crazy ideas at every family gathering. But here's the truth: ideas don't build companies. Execution does.

Vision isn't valuable until someone delivers on it. Strategy means nothing until it's acted on. The difference between successful founders and frustrated ones? The successful founders don't get stuck in the "what ifs". They move into the "what's next". They act while others are still planning their pitch decks, because real progress doesn't happen in the pitch; it happens in the build.

THE MOMENT IT HIT ME: WHY IDEAS AREN'T ENOUGH

I've seen too many brilliant campaigns that never launched and new products that stayed in "research mode". I've watched leaders who wanted to build but never picked a date.

The truth is, the world is full of brilliant thinkers who have never shipped, launched and led. Your ideas don't matter until someone pays for them – until a client uses them, a team delivers them, a system supports them or the market feels them. Until then, they're all just noise.

🧠 MINDSET PRINCIPLE: EXECUTION IS A DISCIPLINE, NOT A TRAIT

Execution isn't about personality. It's not about being a "closer" or having a Type-A mindset.

Execution is about:

- Clarity
- Ownership
- Speed
- Systems
- Urgency
- Culture

If you want to build something that lasts, you need to install execution as an organisational rhythm, not just as a heroic act when you're inspired from time to time.

🛠 FRAMEWORK/PLAYBOOK: MY EXECUTION FRAMEWORK

Here are the five principles I use across my companies to make sure ideas scale and don't stall. I treat execution like engineering. Rather than emotion, ego, hope or hype, it's about turning raw intent into finished impact.

Validate Fast.

Before we build anything, we ask: Is this solving a real problem? Is it urgent, not just a nice-to-have? Can we do it better than the market? If the answer isn't a clear yes, we kill the idea. No ego, no emotions, no attachment – only clarity.

Assign a Leader.

Every project in each of my companies gets a single owner: one person, one name and one deadline. Execution dies in group ownership.

Launch in Three Phases.

Every rollout follows the same rhythm:

- Phase 1 – MVP: Launch fast. Get it working.
- Phase 2 – Polish: Improve the 20% that matters most.
- Phase 3 – Elevate: Make it iconic. Add the "wow".

We don't wait for perfect. We launch with purpose, aiming for excellence and refining as we go.

Define "Done" Before You Start.

We never say, "We're working on it." We ask, "What does 'done' look like, and when will it be delivered?" This one question eliminates 80% of drift and misalignment.

Track and Tweak Weekly.

We don't set and forget. We track progress, feedback, bottlenecks, morale and key metrics. Every project either moves forward or gets realigned – quickly. Execution is measured in movement, not in meetings.

⚠ WARNING SIGN: THE COST OF INCOMPLETE EXECUTION

Most businesses don't fail because of bad ideas. They fail because good ideas are never shipped.

Here's what stalled execution costs your business:

- Culture momentum
- Credibility
- Team belief
- Client trust
- Market opportunity

Every time you delay an idea "until it's ready", you create space for someone else to beat you to the result you were meant to own.

WHAT I TELL MY TEAMS

- "You don't get points for thinking. You get points for outcomes."
- "Execution is how you build trust, inside and out."
- "Don't pitch perfect. Deliver real."
- "If it matters, it moves. If it doesn't, it dies."
- "We don't celebrate potential. We reward delivery."

FIELD NOTES

- The world doesn't remember what you started. It remembers what you finished.
- Speed compounds. Perfection delays.
- A half-executed idea is worse than no idea at all.
- Execution isn't a step. It's the engine.
- No one gets market share for "almost".

🔍 BEHIND THE CHAPTER

I wrote this chapter after reviewing our internal innovation pipeline. We had so many ideas and so much potential, but a handful of those ideas had been floating around for months. There was no owner, no timeline and no movement. Everyone was "still testing", "still refining" and "still aligning".

We had 90% of the work done but zero client impact. That's when I walked in and made it clear: "If this doesn't ship in the next seven days, it's off the table." My decision forced speed, and in the rush to deliver, the team unlocked the clarity they would never have found in planning mode. The launch was messy but powerful. We got real feedback, traction and momentum. And that was the reminder: Ideas rot in draft folders. Execution sharpens in motion.

You don't build empires by "thinking" about them. You build greatness by delivering. If it matters, build it. If it doesn't, delete it. This chapter reinforces a foundational pillar of The Standard System™: **Execution**. Because momentum only begins when ownership, clarity and speed collide.

RAISE THE STANDARD

- What idea have you been talking about but not executed?
- Where is a project drifting because no one owns it?
- What initiative could launch at MVP level this week and improve live?
- What's one decision you've delayed that needs to ship now?

In the next chapter, we explore how the right systems don't restrict freedom but create it.

NOTES

CHAPTER 14

SYSTEMS CREATE FREEDOM

If your business breaks when you step away, you don't have a business – you have a job.

STRATEGIC INSIGHT

By now, you already know that systems matter. In Chapter 4, I shared how I became the bottleneck in my own business and what it took to start letting go. This chapter is about what came next: how I replaced myself.

I've learned the hard way that freedom in business isn't found in absence. It's found in architecture and in systems that scale results, protect standards and evolve without you.

Systems aren't a form of bureaucracy; they're freedom. Without systems, leaders get trapped. They become firefighters, fixers and babysitters. Their calendars fill up, but the company doesn't move without them.

A true system scales standards. It protects quality, empowers people and delivers results without you chasing or checking on your teams.

In Chapter 4, I shared the mindset shift. Now, it's time to introduce the operating manual for making the shift real. Because workable systems don't just support the work; they also replace the need for micromanaging.

🔥 THE MOMENT IT HIT ME: WHEN THIS BECAME NON-NEGOTIABLE

Years ago, a major account escalated a client issue that should have been solved by my team. The problem wasn't bad service; it was inconsistency. Everyone "knew" the process, but nothing was written down. Nothing was tracked or owned.

We didn't lose the client, but we almost lost their trust. It was a turning point. So, we rebuilt everything. We documented, automated and assigned.

Good service can't depend on feeling motivated or being in a "good mood"; it must live in the system and the structure.

🧠 MINDSET PRINCIPLE: WHY SYSTEMS = LEADERSHIP

- Systems protect your brand when you're not in the room.
- They scale consistency without killing culture.
- They allow you to delegate without fear.
- They keep people accountable without micromanagement.
- They create clarity across departments, clients and channels.

If you want to scale anything, you need systems that don't just support you but also replace you.

FRAMEWORK/PLAYBOOK: MY FIVE-PART SYSTEM-BUILDING FRAMEWORK

Define the Outcome.

What must this system deliver every time? Not just the step but also the *result*. If you don't define the outcome, the process becomes opinion-based and collapses under pressure.

Map It Visually.

Every working system should be diagrammable, showing inputs, people, timing, tools and output. If it's too vague to draw, it can't be implemented.

Assign a Single Owner.

Every system gets one name. There's no shared ownership, no "we're all responsible".

Automate or Template Anything That Repeats.

If it repeats, templatise or systemise:

- Client responses
- Escalation handling
- Onboarding
- Reporting
- Internal communications

We don't "wing it" twice.

Review Every 90 Days.

We audit what's outdated, what's working and what's falling behind. If our system hasn't been revisited, it's already decaying.

⚠ WARNING SIGN: THE COST OF NOT SYSTEMISING

Here's what happens when structure is missing:

- Onboarding is inconsistent.
- Client follow-ups rely on memory.
- Issues get lost in email threads.
- You repeat instructions instead of scaling outcomes.
- Talent leaves, because chaos is exhausting.

Worst of all, you stay trapped in work you should have already replaced with an owner or a machine.

💬 WHAT I TELL MY TEAMS

- "If we've solved it twice, it needs a system."
- "You don't scale by fixing problems. You scale by fixing how problems get fixed."
- "The system is the product."
- "No owner, no outcome."
- "Structure creates space. Chaos consumes it."

✍ FIELD NOTES

- Systems don't restrict creativity; they protect consistency.
- Every system that works without you creates capacity *for you*.
- Scale isn't about doing more; it's about designing smarter.
- Systems codify culture. They protect it when you're not in the room.
- Freedom isn't the absence of responsibility; it's the result of structure.

BEHIND THE CHAPTER

This chapter came about after reviewing our internal architecture across multiple companies. Some systems had started to lag, and we had outgrown others. Staff were improvising processes. Clients were getting different experiences depending on who they spoke to. And too many answers lived in people's heads, not in handbooks.

The strongest businesses weren't the ones with the most people. They were the ones with the cleanest systems and the most dedicated owners.

That's when I made it non-negotiable: Every repeating task, every client journey, every pain point must be systemised, documented, tracked, owned and reviewed, or it will eventually break.

This chapter reflects the concepts of **Execution** and **Structure** within The Standard System™. Because freedom isn't the absence of responsibility; it's the result of structure that delivers without your presence, and it's engineered through design.

RAISE THE STANDARD

- What part of your business still depends on your memory or your presence to work?
- What process has never been written down and breaks every time someone's away?
- What system needs a name, a map and a review date, starting this week?
- If you were removed for 30 days, what would hold and what would collapse?

In the next chapter, we set out why pressure, pain and setbacks aren't interruptions but invitations to build smarter, stronger and more strategically.

NOTES

CHAPTER 15

TURNING ADVERSITY INTO STRATEGY

Don't just survive it. Use it.

STRATEGIC INSIGHT

Entrepreneurs often talk about "resilience". Many leaders speak about "overcoming obstacles", but the concept is often misunderstood. Few know how to turn adversity into architecture.

After a crisis, most people bounce back – but "bouncing back" simply gets you back to where you were. If you want to build something unbreakable, you have to bounce forward. It's not just about getting back up; it's also about what you build when you do.

Having learned a number of painful lessons in my life, I've come to believe that adversity is your advantage – if you learn how to mine it. By extracting the insight, building the system and turning the pain into process, **adversity is your audit, and strategy is what you build from the wreckage.**

This chapter is rooted in one of the most overlooked strategies of The Standard System™: **Resilience turned into Structure**. Because real leadership isn't about avoiding pain; it's about designing what comes after it.

THE MOMENT IT HIT ME: MY MOST PAINFUL SEASON BECAME MY SHARPEST STRATEGY

By now, you already know my story: the bike accident, the surgeries, the opioids, the hidden addiction and the gargantuan battle to function.

While the outside world only saw the growth of my business, my internal world was collapsing. I was leading deals, scaling companies and smiling on stage while battling dependency behind closed doors.

But what matters here isn't the pain I went through; it's about what it revealed. The breakthrough didn't come when I recovered but when I started *rebuilding differently*.

I didn't want to revert to the leader I once was. I knew that I had to rewire my approach. So, I asked harder questions, built smarter systems and redesigned my boundaries, rhythms and team dynamics. That season of pain did not merely fortify me but also sharpened *everything*.

MINDSET PRINCIPLE: WHAT ADVERSITY REVEALS

- Systems that weren't built right
- People who weren't truly aligned
- Habits that were unsustainable
- Blind spots you were ignoring

You don't always see it in times of success, but pressure exposes what all the hype and applause hide. And that's where real leadership begins.

🛠 FRAMEWORK/PLAYBOOK: HOW I TURN PAIN INTO PROCESS

Extract the Insight Without the Emotion.
Pain is emotional. Strategy is neutral. I always ask: What failed? What did I miss? What's the actual root cause?

Rebuild the Infrastructure, Not Just the Interface.
Don't patch the surface; reinforce the foundation. If clients leave, replace them – but also rebuild the retention system.

Document the Lesson.
If it's not written, it's repeated. Every failure becomes part of the business playbook.

Use It to Set a New Standard.
Adversity redefines what's acceptable. If the pain was real, the adjustment should be permanent.

⚠ WARNING SIGN: THE COST OF WASTED ADVERSITY

Pain is expensive, but it's also valuable. If you hide it, rush past it or pretend it didn't happen, you're wasting the lessons that arise from it. If you ignore it, the consequences will come back – louder, harsher and more public – unless you learn from the crisis. Every business has failures, but the best ones turn failure into frameworks.

💬 WHAT I TELL MY TEAMS

- “This didn’t happen to us. It happened *for* us, if we use it.”
- “Document the pain. Build from it.”
- “We don’t bounce back; we build forward.”
- “Every pressure point is a system waiting to be installed.”

✍ FIELD NOTES

- Your worst moment can become your best design – if you treat it like data.
- Unprocessed pain leads to repeated patterns.
- Crisis isn’t random; it’s revealing.
- Don’t fix the surface. Rearchitect the system.
- What breaks you, can also build what comes next.

🔍 BEHIND THE CHAPTER

I almost didn’t write this chapter, because it still stings. Some years ago, I was surrounded by a management team I trusted with my life. They were people I had empowered; I even considered some of them friends.

It turned out that they had secretly built a competing business behind my back. By the time I found out, they had stolen intellectual property, leveraged internal resources and tried to siphon off our clients. The betrayal cut deep, but I had to face it head-on.

Things got worse before they got better. A person whom I had once considered a good friend tried to take me down. It was brutal, but it was also one of the most transformative experiences of my career.

I rebuilt everything by establishing:

- New recruitment filters
- Updated performance frameworks
- Refined legal structures
- Improved access protocols
- Cultural onboarding upgrades

Adversity tests you, but it also gives you the blueprint to prevent it from happening again. At the time, this incident felt like a huge betrayal, but it later inspired me to make the business bulletproof.

This chapter reflects the **Resilience-to-Structure** dimension of The Standard System™. Because setbacks aren't inconvenient interruptions; they're invitations to evolve how you build.

RAISE THE STANDARD

- What adversity have you survived but not yet systemised?
- What pain point revealed a design flaw you still haven't fixed?
- Where have you patched a symptom instead of rebuilding the system?
- What insight from your lowest moment could become someone else's playbook?

In the next chapter, we move from adapting under pressure to architecting with intention. We also explore how the most powerful structures are built backwards, with the end always in sight.

NOTES

CHAPTER 16

DESIGN WITH THE END IN MIND

If you don't know where you're going, everything becomes urgent and nothing becomes legendary.

STRATEGIC INSIGHT

Too many businesses are built in survival mode. They get tangled up in:

- Reactive marketing
- Crisis-driven meetings
- Last-minute hiring
- Tactical decisions driven by noise, not vision

It often feels like progress, but it's really just momentum wrapped up in panic. **Great companies aren't built on panicked urgency; they're often built in reverse.**

In my experience, you don't scale greatness with guesswork but by designing with the end in mind. Legendary founders don't just move forward; they also design backwards, always with the prize clearly defined. They build what they want others to inherit, then architect every layer to align with their vision. This chapter reflects the **Legacy-Driven Design** concept within The Standard System™, where everything is built to outlive you.

🔥 THE MOMENT IT HIT ME: WHEN THIS PRINCIPLE WAS FORGED

When I lost my first restaurant in Johannesburg, I was devastated but not surprised. After we were forced to close shop, I spent sleepless nights asking myself what had gone wrong – but deep down, I knew the answer.

We didn't fail because of a lack of passion. We failed because we never defined the destination and the final outcome. There was no long-term structure or vision beyond the month-to-month hustle. We had not designed systems to carry us beyond our limits. We simply kept going until we couldn't any more.

That experience taught me the difference between building to launch and building to last. Since then, every company I've ever built has been strategised and then designed in reverse – by writing the ending first.

🧠 MINDSET PRINCIPLE: WHAT IT MEANS TO DESIGN WITH THE END IN MIND

This isn't about exit planning; it's about architectural clarity.

Before scaling anything, I ask:

- "What will this look like when I'm not running it?"
- "What needs to be documented, delegated or automated now?"
- "If someone else took over, would the brand survive or disappear?"
- "What story should this company tell long after I'm gone?"

If it can't thrive without you, it's not a business – it's a dependency.

🛠 FRAMEWORK/PLAYBOOK: HOW I BUILD FOR WHAT COMES AFTER ME

I Write the Final Scene First.

I journal the outcome in vivid detail. What does the brand feel like at scale? What should the team, systems and client experience look like, even if I am not in the room? Once I can see it, I build toward it.

I Design for Delegation From Day One.

Even if I'm the only one doing the work, I build it like I'll hand it over. If I'm not building for replacement, I'm building for burnout.

I Systemise the Experience, Not Just the Tasks.

Processes matter, but feelings last longer. I map out the emotional rhythm of the customer journey, the tone of our brand voice and the story behind our aesthetic. As I've said over and over again, people remember what you delivered as well as how you made them feel. If they don't feel it, they won't stay.

I Protect the Culture in Writing.

Our values, voice, expectations and onboarding scripts aren't left to memory. They're documented, taught, revisited and refined. Culture doesn't survive through conversation; it survives through codification.

I Design for Exit, Even if I Never Leave.

I may never sell it, but I build every business like I could. This forces clarity, clean financials, bulletproof systems and brand equity. Whether I leave or not isn't the point. What matters is that the exceptional standard outlives me.

⚠ WARNING SIGN: THE RISK OF BUILDING WITHOUT THE END IN MIND

- You trap yourself in the centre.
- You build things that can't be scaled or sold.
- You lead reactively, not strategically.
- You drain your team with urgency instead of building rhythm.
- You confuse momentum with mastery.

Worst of all, you build something that works today but cannot last tomorrow.

💬 WHAT I TELL MY BUILDERS

- "Don't just design for now. Design for when you're gone."
- "Your real job is to build what others can carry."
- "If you disappeared tomorrow, what would break?"
- "The end determines the architecture. Don't skip it."

✍ FIELD NOTES

- Vision without architecture becomes chaos in disguise.
- Culture doesn't scale if it lives only in your head.
- Every business should outgrow you, or it dies with you.
- Urgency fades. Design sustains.
- If the brand dies when you leave, you weren't building. You were babysitting.

🔍 BEHIND THE CHAPTER

This chapter came into focus after I had major back surgery in the United States. I was offline for more than three weeks. I couldn't check in, approve anything or step in to fix a problem.

Even though I was man down and unavailable, when I returned to my desk, my insurance company hadn't just functioned – it had performed. Client queries were handled and operational standards maintained. Nothing collapsed or broke. The business had breathed on its own.

It wasn't simply my good luck. It was the result of years of intentional design: systems, documentation, culture, cadence – all built to operate without my daily presence. That period forced me to really understand a deeper truth: if you're still the engine, you're also the liability.

The experience both validated the structure and proved the philosophy: *You don't build to look busy; you build to leave something behind. And if you want to build something exceptional, you don't start at the beginning – you start with the end in mind and build backwards, always with legacy in mind.*

RAISE THE STANDARD

- What part of your business still depends on your presence to function?
- If you handed it over today, what would hold and what would collapse?
- Where are you designing for survival instead of scale?
- What future state should you define now so you can build towards it?

Before we move on to Chapter 17, let's first recap Part II.

NOTES

PART II RECAP – STRUCTURE: BUILD WHAT LASTS

You don't scale by doing more. You scale by building what moves without you.

This section wasn't about policies, checklists or processes for the sake of documentation. It was about *structural intelligence* – the kind of architecture that sustains your standard long after you've stepped out of the room.

The real test of leadership isn't what you build when you're present; it's what keeps performing when you're not. Structure gives your vision weight. It removes chaos. It distributes ownership, protects consistency and scales trust.

The chapters in this section form the **operational spine** of The Standard System™. They are all designed to make greatness repeatable.

WHAT YOU'VE JUST MASTERED

Chapter 7: From Culture to Reputation

Culture is the internal brand. Reputation is what the market repeats. If there's misalignment between the two, the brand collapses in chaos or silence.

Chapter 8: Creating a Culture of Accountability

If no one owns it, nothing moves. Accountability isn't pressure; it's momentum. Every deliverable needs a name, a deadline and a finish line.

Chapter 9: Leading With Vision, Not Ego

Ego builds control. Vision builds companies. You don't scale by being the hero. You scale by stepping back and building others to replace you.

Chapter 10: The Most Powerful Word in Business

An apology isn't a PR tactic. It's a leadership move. Owning your mistakes early and visibly, builds more trust than strategy ever will.

Chapter 11: The EQ Standard

Emotional intelligence isn't soft. It's structural. It's what holds the culture, sharpens the tone, and leads the room when pressure spikes and clarity matters most.

Chapter 12: Empowering the Next Generation

Legacy lives in people. The builders you develop are the only scalable proof of your leadership.

Chapter 13: From Idea to Execution

You won't be remembered for what you planned but for what you delivered. Execution isn't a trait; it's a system.

Chapter 14: Systems Create Freedom

You can't scale chaos. Structure creates clarity, consistency and the ability to lead without being needed.

Chapter 15: Turning Adversity Into Strategy

Every setback is an audit. If you document and rebuild, pain becomes infrastructure. If you don't, it repeats and breaks you and your business.

Chapter 16: Design With the End in Mind

If the brand can't survive without you, you're not building – you're babysitting. Real builders start with the legacy and design backwards.

YOUR STRUCTURAL AUDIT: EIGHT QUESTIONS TO REFLECT ON

- Where am I still the bottleneck in my company's process flow?
- What do I need to stop "managing" and start systemising?
- Which outcome is drifting because there's no single owner?
- Who on my team is ready to lead but still being treated like a follower?
- Which ideas have I been sitting on that should already be live?
- Which inconsistencies in service or delivery are eroding our reputation?
- Where have I survived pain but not yet built from it?
- What would this business need to look like in order to outlive me?

THE SHIFT

Structure isn't restrictive; it's liberating.

The right structure removes emotional decision-making. It distributes clarity and scales the founder's DNA without burning it out.

Part II gave you the tools to move from mindlessly "doing" to strategically designing; from being a leader that holds things together to being a leader that builds what others carry forward.

Now the question is simple: What still depends on you, and what would freedom look like if it didn't?

It's time for Part III, on culture and energy and why these are so important when you're building your standards.

NOTES

PART III

CULTURE & ENERGY: WHY IT MATTERS

CHAPTER 17

ENERGY IS THE ADVANTAGE

Skills get the job done. Energy changes the room.

STRATEGIC INSIGHT

In business, energy is the real differentiator – not just physical but emotional, cultural and brand energy. It's not just something you claim; it's something people feel. Before prospective clients understand your product or hear your pitch, they sense your presence. You can have the best logo, the slickest campaign and the most premium product, but if the energy is off, people won't trust you. They won't refer you and they won't come back, even if they can't explain why.

Brands don't only fail because of poor strategy, but also because of poor energy. **And in a crowded market, your brand's energy is your loudest competitive edge.**

THE MOMENT IT HIT ME: HOW I LEARNED THIS THE HARD WAY

Nothing saps energy more than being in the grip of addiction. During the five years I spent seesawing between opioid withdrawal and dependence, I lost my life force. I couldn't find the version of myself who had once loved business, leadership and momentum. As my addiction intensified, there were days when I wondered whether I wouldn't be better off dead.

On the surface, the world thought I was winning: the business was growing, the brand was expanding and the team was performing. But in reality, I felt like a zombie. I'd walk into meetings feeling completely numb. Everything looked right on the outside, but I felt out of sync. I might have been delivering, but I wasn't connecting.

One morning, I looked in the mirror. The reflection that stared back at me was a ghost of my former self. I couldn't stomach what I saw. That's when I realised, come hell or high water, I had to find a way out of this agony and get my energy back. And so, my long journey of recovery began, one hour and one day at a time.

Losing my energy made me understand how valuable it truly was. Now that I'm free from addiction and I've recovered from the burnout that came with it, I don't just protect my energy – I engineer it into everything I build.

MINDSET PRINCIPLE: WHAT ENERGY REALLY IS

- It's how your team responds when you walk in.
- It's what your client feels before the proposal lands.
- It's the rhythm of your culture between meetings, handovers and deadlines.
- It's the way your business *feels* when no one's performing but everything's still moving.
- Energy is the emotional tone of your execution. It either inspires trust or quietly erodes it.

🛠️ FRAMEWORK/PLAYBOOK: HOW I PROTECT AND ENGINEER ENERGY

I Guard My Inputs.

You are shaped by what you consume. So, I filter who I follow, what I read and what enters my headspace. I avoid gossip and unnecessary dramas.

I Lead With High Frequency.

If I walk in drained or reactive, that's the culture I transfer. So, I train, fuel and reset. Energy doesn't just come from effort; it comes from intention too.

I Design Environments That Lift.

Every business I run is engineered for a vibe:

- Lighting
- Sound
- Scent
- Layout
- Flow

These aren't design choices. They're emotional performance tools.

I Start With Emotion, Not With Assets.

We reverse-engineer everything based on one question: What should this experience feel like, from start to finish? Then we build the systems, training and touchpoints around that feeling.

I Script Key Transitions.

We don't leave first impressions to chance. We map the energy of:

- Entry
- Welcome
- Interaction
- Exit
- Follow-up

Every transition is an emotional anchor. If we don't feel it, neither will our clients.

I Train People to Be Energy Carriers.

It's not about being extroverted but about being emotionally present. We train:

- Posture
- Tone
- Eye contact
- Pacing
- Presence in silence

Because your people are the brand.

I Audit the Atmosphere.

Every 90 days, I walk through my businesses and ask:

- What feels off?
- What's draining the room?
- Are our people present or just performing?
- Is the energy sharp or just polished?

I do the same with myself, because I now know that burnout is feedback, and disconnection is a warning. So, when my energy drops, I don't wait for the crash. I make sure to recover it before the burnout happens. I've truly come to believe that energy is currency, and these days, I spend it wisely.

⚠ WARNING SIGN: THE SILENT THREAT OF FLAT ENERGY

Low energy doesn't announce itself. Rather, it silently whispers:

- "That's not my job."
- "I'll deal with it later."
- "I'm here, but I'm not really here."

Burnout doesn't crush you overnight. Instead, it bleeds you slowly until you start resenting what you've built, questioning what you're doing and losing the presence that once made you magnetic. The worst part is that you might still look like you're winning, even when you're feeling nothing at all.

🗨 WHAT I TELL MY TEAMS

- "Bring energy, or protect it, but don't drain it."
- "Your tone is your brand."
- "You don't need to be loud; you need to be charged."
- "No one follows a flatline."
- "Energy leads everything."
- "If you're exhausted, rest – don't retreat."

✍ FIELD NOTES

- Energy isn't a personality trait; it's a performance multiplier.
- Brands aren't built on logos; they're built on emotional memory.
- People remember how you made them *feel* long after they forget what you delivered.
- Flat energy kills trust quietly.
- If your culture feels off, check the frequency, not just the structure.

BEHIND THE CHAPTER

This chapter took shape after I had entered one of our boardrooms and felt the energy drop the second the next person entered. He was brilliant at his job, technically sound and had top-level skills, but he was draining the team. He couldn't communicate. He dominated conversations. He thought his presence held the department together. Turns out, nearly everyone on his team wanted to resign because of him. He didn't fail because of incompetence; he failed because of his misaligned energy. That's when I realised: **Culture doesn't just follow clarity; it also follows energy.**

These days, I treat energy as a KPI. We track it, train for it and protect it – across every floor, every meeting and every leadership layer. Because when the energy is right, execution sharpens, trust grows and the entire brand hums.

RAISE THE STANDARD

- What's draining your team more than you realise?
- What space in your business needs an energy audit this week?
- Who in your leadership team is technically strong but emotionally tone-deaf?
- What's one environmental or emotional upgrade you can engineer this month?

In the next chapter, we explore one of the hardest emotional shifts in leadership: letting go of control without losing the brand you've worked so hard to build.

NOTES

CHAPTER 18

THE FOUNDER'S DILEMMA

If you don't let go, you can't scale. If you let go blindly, you lose the brand. It's all about letting go without losing control.

STRATEGIC INSIGHT

All founders eventually hit a wall – not because they lack drive, but because they refuse to release control. I've touched on this in an earlier chapter, but it's extremely important to expand on this idea.

It's not easy letting go when you've built something from the ground up. You know every detail, and you've spent years protecting it with everything you've got. So, when it's time to delegate, a question haunts you: "Will they care for it like I do?"

And that's the dilemma. Because if you hold on too tightly, you burn out and bottleneck the business. But if you let go too freely, you risk watching everything slip below the standard you've worked so hard to establish.

The answer isn't more or less control, or more or less trust. It's all about better design.

🔥 THE MOMENT IT HIT ME: WHEN I REALISED I HAD TO LET GO

As I've mentioned in previous chapters, there was a time when every decision in the business ran through me: every hire, every campaign and every final call. It made me feel important and essential – even irreplaceable. But deep down, I knew it was unsustainable.

The wake-up moment came during a leadership meeting I almost didn't attend. I'd been overwhelmed and distracted, and I was running on fumes. One of my team leaders challenged a strategic decision to which I was emotionally attached and proposed a better path forward. She'd seen something I hadn't. She was right – and I wasn't.

The team backed her. Her solution was sharper than mine. And it worked. I sat there, stunned. Not because they didn't need me, but because I realised they shouldn't *always* need me. That moment taught me something vital: Real leadership isn't about control – it's about multiplication. You don't let go because you're tired. You let go because you've built something strong enough to stand without you.

🧠 MINDSET PRINCIPLE: WHY FOUNDERS STRUGGLE TO LET GO

Fear of Decline

"If I let go, the standard will drop."

Fear of Irrelevance

"If they don't need me, what's my value?"

Fear of Being Burned Again
"I've trusted people before, and it cost me."

These fears are real. But so is this truth: **The more central you remain, the less scalable you become.**

🛠 FRAMEWORK/PLAYBOOK: HOW I LET GO WITHOUT LOSING THE BRAND

Systemise First. Delegate Second.
You can't delegate chaos, so every process gets:

- A visual map
- A checklist or dashboard
- A feedback loop
- A defined outcome

I don't delegate tasks. I delegate systems.

Define the "Why" Behind the Work.
If people only understand the *task*, they'll protect *productivity*. If they understand the *meaning*, they'll protect the *mission*.

Train Replacements, Not Assistants.
I don't want people who need my input. I want people who *replace my input with better thinking*.

Stay Close Without Being Controlling.
I don't disappear. Instead, I monitor outcomes, not effort, and lead through dashboards and rhythm and cultural pulse checks.

Shift From Operator to Architect.
I no longer run the system. I design the vision, maintain the

rhythm and protect the energy. That's the difference between *letting go* and *leading forward*.

⚠ WARNING SIGN: THE COST OF STAYING AT THE CENTRE

- Decisions slow down.
- Confidence shrinks.
- People stop taking the initiative.
- The brand becomes shaky because it only works when you're in the room.

Control feels efficient, but it's a short-term illusion. Letting go *the right way* is the only long-term strategy that works.

💬 WHAT I TELL FOUNDERS

- "You don't need to control everything to protect the brand."
- "Your job isn't to run the machine; it's to refine the engine."
- "If your team can't move without you, you haven't built a business – you've built a bottleneck."
- "Let go by creating systems, not by keeping silent."

✍ FIELD NOTES

- Founders who remain too central become ceilings.
- Systems are how you release control without releasing standards.
- Letting go without design is reckless. With design, it's leadership.
- The strongest companies don't need their founders ever-present; they reflect them in every process.
- You don't lose your legacy by letting go. You lose it by refusing to.

BEHIND THE CHAPTER

I wrote this after watching a leader on my team making a decision I didn't agree with and realising she was right. It was during a period of change across the business. I was pushing hard – too hard. My pace was creating fear and insecurity among some of my team members.

This leader slowed things down. She challenged my thinking and made the decision her way. She didn't ask for my input, but she followed the standard I'd set and even improved on it.

She didn't need me. She didn't check with me. She led without me, and it worked. It was exactly what I had trained her to do. This was an internal shift where I realised: You're not letting go of control; you're installing trust. When done correctly, it doesn't reduce your influence – it multiplies it.

RAISE THE STANDARD

- Where are you holding on – not because it's required but because it feels safe?
- What system could you build this week to release control without releasing consistency?
- Who on your team is ready to lead if you'd let them?
- What would change if you started leading like an architect instead of an operator?

In the next chapter, we bring it all home by focusing on legacies and systems built to outlast the one who built them.

NOTES

CHAPTER 19

BUILD ONCE, USE FOREVER

If you're solving the same problem twice, you've already lost.

STRATEGIC INSIGHT

Many business leaders waste time not because they're lazy but because they keep solving the same problem over and over again. They rewrite the same email, re-explain the same processes, retrain after the same mistakes and keep answering the same questions. This is not leadership. It's inefficiency disguised as effort.

Great builders don't just complete the work; they also turn it into an asset. They build it once, then use it as leverage.

THE MOMENT IT HIT ME: THE DAY I GOT TIRED OF REPEATING MYSELF

My lightbulb moment was triggered by a claims process. Every time a complex claim came in, my team would spend hours:

- Debating which loss adjuster or specialist to appoint
- Writing custom update emails from scratch
- Managing escalations manually
- Resolving the same misunderstandings over and over again

It was frustrating and unnecessary, and I realised that it was my fault because I hadn't built repeatable processes around it. We weren't inefficient because of incompetence; we were inefficient because we hadn't built a system.

I then made a new rule: If we do something more than twice, we capture it, systemise it and scale it.

This rule has saved us hundreds of hours a month and significantly sharpened our client experience.

🧠 MINDSET PRINCIPLE: WHAT IT MEANS TO BUILD ONCE, USE FOREVER

This mindset shifts you from:
- Solving → Structuring
- Explaining → Enabling
- Reacting → Scaling

You start turning:
- Actions into assets
- Answers into templates
- Wins into frameworks
- Errors into systems

And you begin compounding time instead of consuming it.

🛠 FRAMEWORK/PLAYBOOK: HOW I CODIFY REPEATABLE EXCELLENCE

Turn execution into infrastructure.
We don't simply finish tasks. We ask: *Can this be reused?* If the answer is yes, it gets systemised.

Create Reusable Templates for Everything.
If it repeats, it gets templated with:
- Proposal decks
- Internal updates
- Staff onboarding
- Client handovers
- Team check-ins

There is no freestyling where consistency matters.

Document in Motion.
We don't wait to build manuals in isolation. We document as we go – via Loom, screenshots, checklists and debriefs.

Speed + context = living systems.

Build Libraries, Not Legends.
If only one person knows how it works, it's not a system – it's a liability. We build central, searchable resources that survive departures, promotions and burnout.

Review and Refine Quarterly.
Every 90 days, we walk the system and ask:
- Is this still working?
- What's being skipped or bypassed?
- What's outdated or unclear?

Static systems die. Living systems evolve.

⚠ WARNING SIGN: THE COST OF NOT CAPTURING

Every time you:

- Re-answer a question
- Redesign a document
- Rehandle a fix
- Re-explain a decision

You waste:

- Time
- Trust
- Consistency
- Momentum
- Long-term scalability

You also increase dependencies on people instead of empowering performance through process.

💬 WHAT I TELL MY TEAMS

- "If we've solved it twice, we capture it."
- "Don't just complete it. Codify it."
- "If it repeats, it gets a system."
- "Your genius isn't in what you know; it's in what you leave behind."
- "Build once. Use forever. Then refine."

✍ FIELD NOTES

- Operational leverage is built, not hoped for.
- You don't scale output. You scale inputs through systems.
- Reusability reduces stress, increases consistency and multiplies time.

- Documentation is how culture survives turnover.
- If your excellence lives in people's heads, it dies in their absence.

🔍 BEHIND THE CHAPTER

I wrote this chapter after reviewing four separate client escalations, similar in nature but handled by different team members. They all did a great job, but each one started from scratch. There were no shared responses, process memory or templates – just a group of capable people burning energy to solve the same type of issue repeatedly.

That's when I snapped – not at the team but at the inefficiency. It wasn't just time being wasted – it was trust; trust in each other, in our consistency and in the idea that we were operating like a company, not merely passing the baton in a never-ending relay. So, I made this a rule:
If it works, we capture it.
If it repeats, we build a system.
If it matters, we teach it.

This single mindset shift has saved us thousands of hours. It has protected our brand and reduced drag in every division.

It's how you stop being "busy" and start becoming bulletproof.

📝 RAISE THE STANDARD

- What process, fix or insight have you repeated when it should already be a system?
- Where is operational genius still trapped in someone's head?
- What documentation could you build this week that buys back hours in the next 12 months?
- What system, template or framework needs to go from "done" to "repeatable"?

In the next chapter, we move from reusability to reputation and explore why brand energy lives in what your people feel long before they remember what you've delivered.

NOTES

CHAPTER 20

REPUTATION IS THE REAL BRAND

Your brand isn't what you say. It's what people say when you're not in the room.

STRATEGIC INSIGHT

You can spend millions on logos, build the most beautiful websites and craft the cleverest campaigns, but if the experience doesn't match the promise, you've already lost your clients' trust. I can't say this often enough: People may not remember your tagline, your offer or your exact words, but they will always remember how your brand made them *feel*. Reputation is not built on your marketing. It's built on how you behave under pressure, not just how you shine during the pitch. Reputation is forged in the emotional aftermath of every interaction, and it reflects your internal state more than you think.

THE MOMENT IT HIT ME: THE POWER OF CONSISTENCY

One day, I walked into a boardroom to pitch to a major broker. Before I could speak, their CEO leaned in and said, "Your reputation arrived ten minutes before you did."

That's when I realised that consistency isn't just discipline; it's also marketing.

He hadn't seen our deck or heard our pitch. But he'd felt our reputation before I even opened my mouth. That moment taught me something I'll never forget: **Your brand starts long before your pitch, and it lasts long after your marketing campaign ends.**

🧠 MINDSET PRINCIPLE: WHAT REPUTATION IS ACTUALLY BUILT ON

- The tone of your emails
- The sharpness of your follow-through
- The clarity of your "no" and the credibility of your "yes"
- The posture of your team when no one is watching
- The way you respond under pressure

It's not about perfection. It's about *predictability*. People trust what they can count on. Reputation is the result of showing up *the same way* every time.

🛠️ FRAMEWORK/PLAYBOOK: HOW I PROTECT REPUTATION LIKE IT'S CURRENCY

We Train for Pressure Moments.

Reputation isn't built during the easy wins. It's built when things go wrong, and in how you respond.

We train for breakdowns because that's where our brand is protected or erased.

We Don't Let the Promise Drift.

Every touchpoint is a promise. If the tone, timing or clarity fades, we reset – fast.

We Fix the Feeling, Not Just the Problem.

Recovery isn't enough. Trust is rebuilt by addressing *how the client felt,* not only by what went wrong.

We Overdeliver Quietly.

We don't overpromise. We overdeliver on purpose and without the spotlight.

We Own Mistakes Publicly and Early.

Reputation isn't built on being flawless. It's built on owning flaws fast and solving them with power.

⚠ WARNING SIGN: THE COST OF REPUTATION DRIFT

Reputation doesn't collapse overnight. It leaks away slowly because of:

- A delayed follow-up
- A vague reply
- A cold interaction
- An apology that lacks empathy

And suddenly, the client feels *something's changed*. But they usually won't say it; they'll just start doing business elsewhere.

When trust fades, loyalty disappears quietly.

💬 WHAT I TELL MY TEAMS

- "Your actions are our marketing."
- "People don't remember what we pitched. They remember how we made them feel."
- "Protect the promise, even when it's hard."
- "Reputation travels faster than sales."
- "We don't talk brand. We *live* brand."

✍ FIELD NOTES

- Reputation is the trust you earn in your absence.
- You can't fake consistency.
- Branding is what you say. Reputation is what they believe.
- Clients don't chase perfect. They follow dependable.
- If you want referrals, protect the emotional footprint of every touchpoint.

🔍 BEHIND THE CHAPTER

This chapter was born from two sentences I'll never forget: "We didn't choose you because of your proposal. We chose you because of what people said after it."

That moment entirely changed how I think about brand. It reminded me that your reputation is *always ahead of you*. If you don't honour it, something else will replace it. It's not about perfection. It's about *alignment*. I always remind my teams to ask:

- Does the way your team show up match your values?
- Does your tone reinforce your promise?
- Does your follow-through back up your pitch?

People don’t wait for you to explain your intentions; they feel them – and then they tell others.

These days, I don’t just focus on being impressive but also on being consistent. Because consistency is what compounds trust, and trust builds brands that outlast hype.

RAISE THE STANDARD

- What’s one moment in your client journey that feels misaligned even if it seems polished?
- Where are small inconsistencies creating silent drift in trust?
- What’s one reputation-defining moment you can pre-empt this month?
- What would change if your team treated every email, handover or reply as your brand?

In the next chapter, we explore what it really takes to bounce back and why your credibility as a leader is forged not by charisma but by how you move through your lowest moments.

NOTES

CHAPTER 21

THE ART OF THE COMEBACK

The fall doesn't define you. What you build after it does.

STRATEGIC INSIGHT

Most leaders look capable when things are good, when the numbers are up, when the team is aligned and when everything is working. But leadership isn't tested in the win but in the *wreckage*. It's tested in the fall, in the losses, in the moment when everything you used to rely on – discipline, reputation and energy – disappears. That's where the comeback begins. Not as a public victory or show and tell, but as a private rebuild. Because real leaders don't bounce back. **They bounce forward.**

Winners don't pretend it didn't happen. They don't sugarcoat the pain. They use it, mine it and transform through it. That's the art of the comeback.

THE MOMENT IT HIT ME: MY GREATEST COMEBACK DIDN'T HAPPEN ON A STAGE

It happened in a quiet room as I was finally getting off opioids after a monstrous, five-year struggle.

When I started tapering off my buprenorphine intake, there was no grand moment, applause or motivational speeches. There was just pain, persistence and the quiet, invisible decision to keep going. I didn't feel strong or worthy, but I followed my tapering schedule. Millimetre by millimetre, I moved towards my goal: to be free of my addiction at last. I trained my body and honoured the process, even when my mind begged me to stop.

Finally, after years of hell, I realised I wasn't the same man any more and never would be again. Addiction doesn't just take something from you, it rewires you – but if you let it, it also erases what no longer serves you.

Once I was clean, I was sharper, stronger and stripped of ego. I was clearer than I had ever been before my accident. That's what moving through pain gave me – not recovery, but reinvention. That's the art of the comeback: not a return, but a rebirth.

MINDSET PRINCIPLE: WHAT EVERY COMEBACK REQUIRES

Radical Ownership

There must be no blame, no spin and no great heroic narrative. Rather embrace taking full responsibility for what happened and what comes next.

Truth Without Drama

You don't need to exaggerate the pain. Just face it and ask:

- What happened?
- What did I ignore?
- What must change forever?

A New Operating System

You don't get to return to who you were. That version is gone, so you build a new mindset, structure and rhythm.

Irrational Discipline

Comebacks aren't powered by hype. They're powered by micro-decisions stacked daily, like Kaizen – the Japanese business philosophy that encourages incremental changes for the better – in its most painful, personal form.

A Redefined Identity

You don't reclaim the old you. You become someone who wouldn't have existed without the fall.

⚠ WARNING SIGN: THE LIE OF LINEAR GROWTH

We love polished timelines, progress charts and public celebrations. But real leadership doesn't work in straight lines. It rises in:

- Tears behind closed doors
- Showing up when no one claps
- Doing the work when you've lost all momentum
- Choosing the standard – even when you feel like a fraud

Scars don't weaken leaders. **They *prove* them.**

💬 WHAT I TELL MY TEAMS

- "You don't need to be perfect. You need to move."
- "Comebacks aren't loud. They're disciplined."
- "If you're at the bottom, good. There's solid ground to rebuild from."
- "You don't have to go back. You can rise *anew*."

✍ FIELD NOTES

- You don't rise into who you were. You rise into who you weren't ready to be.
- Comebacks are often quiet, lonely and full of resistance.
- Pain is the tuition. Discipline is the vehicle.
- Every fall contains the framework for your next standard.
- The most credible leaders are the ones who bled for it but kept moving.

🔍 BEHIND THE CHAPTER

I didn't really want to share this addiction story again, but I wrote it to inspire the founder who's still struggling – the one who's delivering results but dying inside; the one who's managing pressure by hiding pain; those who think they have to lead with perfection when all they really need is the strength to keep showing up. If that sounds familiar, then this chapter is especially for you. It's to remind you that you're not broken; you're just being reforged. Comebacks don't start with applause; they start with brutal honesty and one small, defiant decision: I will rise.

RAISE THE STANDARD

- What pain are you still hiding that could become your power?
- What rhythm, system or identity needs to be rebuilt after your lowest season?
- Where have you been stuck in "recovery mode" when it's time to redesign?
- What would it look like to move – not as who you were, but as who you've now earned the right to be?

Now, let's recap what you learned in Part III.

NOTES

🔁 PART III RECAP – CULTURE & ENERGY: WHY IT MATTERS

People don't remember what you said. They remember what they felt when you built it.

You can have the sharpest systems, the most scalable structure and the clearest strategy in the market, but *if the energy is off*, the culture will crack. And when culture cracks, everything else gets harder.

Part III wasn't about perks or branding. It was about *emotional infrastructure* – the atmosphere that surrounds every message, meeting, client touchpoint and moment of execution.

This section revealed the truth that many leaders miss: **Culture isn't a poster. Energy isn't a vibe. They're both engineered standards. If not, they drift.**

📌 WHAT YOU'VE JUST MASTERED

Chapter 17: Energy is the Advantage

Energy is strategy. It's how your brand moves, your people feel and your clients decide – often before a single word is spoken.

Chapter 18: The Founder's Dilemma

Letting go doesn't mean lowering the bar. It means building the system that *protects the bar without you.*

Chapter 19: Build Once, Use Forever

Don't just solve problems; also codify the solution. Reusability creates reliability and frees your future.

Chapter 20: Reputation is the Real Brand

Reputation is what the market repeats when you're not in the room. If you don't protect it, you can't scale it.

Chapter 21: The Art of the Comeback

Real leadership is forged in the fire. Pain isn't just something you survive; it's what reinvents you.

YOUR CULTURE & ENERGY AUDIT: FIVE QUESTIONS TO REFLECT ON

- Where is low energy draining high performance in your company, and what's the source?
- What part of your culture is still being powered by proximity, not process?
- What pain or setback have you grown through but not yet rebuilt from?
- What system, message or moment isn't aligned with the emotional tone of your brand?
- If your business lost its founder tomorrow, would the energy still feel the same?

THE SHIFT

"Culture" is not a department. "Energy" is not a personality trait. They're both strategic assets that grow every day.

This section has given you the tools to shape how your business *feels* to your team, your clients and your market. Because culture isn't what's said; it's what people protect. And energy is what people *carry* when they leave the room.

As we move to Part IV, the following chapter zooms out from personal resilience to long-term perspective and explores what it takes to design a business that will outlast your presence.

NOTES

PART IV

SCALING, LEGACY & IMPACT

CHAPTER 22

WHEN RISK PAYS OFF

Risk is the price of building anything worthwhile

STRATEGIC INSIGHT

Risk is often treated as something to avoid – a liability, a gamble or a threat. But in leadership, the real threat is usually the opposite: avoidance, overanalysis and hesitation. The most dangerous move is not a bold one; it's a delayed one. You don't grow from the safe zone. You don't lead from the middle lane. And you don't build anything exceptional by only choosing the odds you can guarantee.

The cost of risk may be discomfort, but the cost of not taking risks is far worse:

- Stalled businesses
- Missed opportunities
- Safe decisions that become expensive regrets

You don't have to take reckless risks, but if you want to build something worthwhile, you have to bet on yourself before anyone else does.

🔥 THE MOMENT IT HIT ME: AN UNCALCULATED RISK

In the beginning, my dream to build an empire wasn't calculated or sophisticated. It was raw.

At the age of 23, I left a cushy job at a top brokerage with no guarantees, no backing and no Plan B. I just knew I couldn't keep building someone else's dream.

Everyone around me thought I was reckless. Some smiled politely, assuming I'd come back once I'd "matured". But deep down, I knew that staying was the bigger risk. It might have meant safety, but it also meant stagnation – and I wasn't wired for that.

When I submitted my resignation letter, I had no pitch deck, no exit strategy and no clear roadmap. I simply hungered for something bigger and something even more dangerous than uncertainty. I had absolute clarity: I had outgrown my role. What I lacked in business experience, I made up for in conviction. What I lacked in strategy, I made up for in movement. And, looking back now, taking that uncalculated risk was the most important step of all – not because it was smart, but because it was mine.

🧠 MINDSET PRINCIPLE: RISK REQUIRES MOVEMENT

Calculated risk is a privilege, but courageous risk is a requirement.

The first step won't always be smart, safe or well-timed, but it will be yours – and that's what separates the builders from the bystanders. Most people lose momentum not because they made the wrong move but because they waited too long to make any move at all.

🛠 FRAMEWORK/PLAYBOOK: HOW I MAKE RISK WORK FOR ME

Over the years, I've evolved from an instinctive risk-taker to a strategic risk engineer. Today, I approach risk like a muscle – one that's developed, not inherited.

I Act Before I'm "Ready".
I don't wait for 100% clarity, because I've learned that the magic usually lives at 70%. The final 30% comes in motion through feedback, failure and iteration.

I Filter for Asymmetric Risk.
Every opportunity I evaluate now runs through one core question: Is the upside worth ten times the downside, and is the downside survivable? If yes, I move.

I Make Speed a Strategic Advantage.
We launch at 80%, gather live feedback and sharpen in public. Perfection delays, but speed compounds. Early action buys early traction.

I Build with Builders, Not Bystanders.
Nothing kills risk-taking faster than fear-driven consensus. That's why I choose people who move, adapt and learn out loud. We don't penalise smart mistakes. We penalise safety disguised as intelligence.

⚠ WARNING SIGN: THE COST OF NOT TAKING RISK

Most businesses don't fail because they took the wrong risk. They fail because they took none at all.

Hesitation doesn't look dangerous, at first. But here's what it quietly costs:

- The product you never launched
- The market you never entered
- The talent you never trusted
- The opportunity you didn't grab when the window was open

Hesitation doesn't scream; it whispers. And by the time you realise the moment is gone, someone else has already claimed the space you were waiting to make perfect.

💬 WHAT I TELL MY TEAMS

- "We don't wait for certainty. We lead with conviction."
- "You can't build anything great from the middle lane."
- "Calculated risks come after courageous ones."
- "If it feels uncomfortable, it might be your next breakthrough."
- "Safe is expensive. Fast is strategic."

✍ FIELD NOTES

- Risk is the entrance fee for building anything extraordinary.
- Paralysis isn't safe; it's expensive.
- Momentum doesn't come from spreadsheets; it comes from decisions.

- Hesitation compounds faster than any bad bet.
- Legacy doesn't reward caution; it rewards courage.

BEHIND THE CHAPTER

I wrote this chapter thinking back to the day I left my job at the brokerage with absolutely no backup plan, just the gut feeling that if I didn't bet on myself then, I probably never would.

That decision wasn't strategic; it was instinct. But it became the seed of everything I've built since, because momentum doesn't start with certainty – it starts with courage.

Since that bold and brash move, I've learned how to calculate risk. I've built models, stress-tested ideas and matured as a strategist. But none of it would have mattered if I hadn't taken that first leap.

I've also seen what happens when people don't leap, when they wait too long or when they let hesitation become policy. The opportunity passes, the team disengages and the window doesn't reopen.

The cost of not taking risks doesn't hit your income statement. It hits your trajectory. It shows up in missed growth, a flat culture and the haunting thought that someone else seized the chance you were too cautious to take.

RAISE THE STANDARD

- Where in your business or your life are you overanalysing instead of acting?
- What risk have you avoided that's now costing you momentum?
- What move would you make this week if you backed yourself fully?
- Where have you mistaken hesitation for strategy?
- What opportunity needs to be taken before it feels ready?

In the next chapter, we move from taking risks to the customer service manifesto.

NOTES

CHAPTER 23

THE CUSTOMER SERVICE MANIFESTO

Service isn't a department. It's the brand in action.

STRATEGIC INSIGHT

As mentioned in a previous chapter, you can have the best technology, the most polished website and the most iconic branding in your industry, but if your clients feel ignored, rushed, confused or undervalued, you've already lost them.

Service isn't what happens after the sale. It's the sum of every interaction before, during and after. It's not about solving a problem and moving on; it's about making people feel valued in the process. And in a world driven by AI and too much hype and noise, what people remember most, isn't what you said – it's how you made them feel, especially when things didn't go according to plan.

THE MOMENT IT HIT ME: WHY SOME COMPANIES GET THIS WRONG

Some companies treat service like a department: a help desk, a call centre or a script. They think it's something someone else handles. They build great brands, and then hand the experience over to teams that haven't been taught how to carry and nurture the brand. Clients then feel like numbers. Their frustrations are met with scripts. Their problems remain unresolved, and their brand loyalty dissipates because service is what people notice when they're at their most vulnerable.

Real service is embedded in every detail. It's cultural, strategic and emotional. It's how people feel when they deal with your brand. It's how your team shows up, in tone, speed, attitude and attention. And it creates your reputation.

MINDSET PRINCIPLE: WHAT TRUE SERVICE LOOKS LIKE

It shows up in:

- The tone of your email
- The timing of your follow-up
- The way you say "no" without making someone feel rejected
- The level of care your team brings on a Monday morning after a busy weekend
- The consistency of your attention *after* the payment clears

It's not about being flawless. It's about being *fully present*. Service is emotional architecture, and if you build it right, it becomes the most profitable part of your brand.

FRAMEWORK/PLAYBOOK: THE TEN LAWS OF SERVICE

Serve With Sincerity, Not Scripts.

If it sounds fake, it is. People recognise integrity and authenticity, and they can feel when it's missing.

Make Them Feel Like They're the Only One.
There is only one boss – the customer. And they can fire everybody in the company, from the CEO down, simply by spending their money somewhere else. Even if you serve 10 000 clients, the one in front of you should feel like they're the only one that matters.

Take Ownership, Fast.
Even when it's not your fault, claim the error. Trust is built through action, not deflection.

Fix the Feeling, Not Just the Issue.
Resolution is transactional. Emotional repair is transformational. Your most unhappy customers are your greatest source of learning.

Personalise the Experience.
Use names, remember the context and anticipate needs. Customers don't want to communicate with a computer. They want to talk to a real, live, responsive person who will listen and help them. Automation should never replace human effort – it should enhance it.

Respect Their Time as if It's Yours.
Silence, vague timelines and unclear responses send a loud message: "You're not a priority."

Simplify Everything.
Confusion is friction. Complexity is disrespect. Clarity is care.

Follow Up Without Being Asked.
Proactivity builds credibility. The best follow-up happens after the resolution, when most brands go quiet.

Train From the Inside Out.

Your team can't deliver care they've never experienced. If you can't serve your colleagues, you have no chance of serving your customers. Culture sets the tone, and systems ensure it's repeatable.

Surprise Them on Purpose.

Service is amplified by small, unexpected touches. Kindness isn't scalable, but *thoughtfulness* is.

⚠ WARNING SIGN: THE COST OF TRANSACTIONAL SERVICE

When your team thinks:

- "Just close the ticket."
- "Solve it and move on."
- "Push them to the next step."

Then you don't have a client anymore; you have a countdown to losing one. People stay loyal to how you make them *feel*. It's not what you sold to them or promised them, but what they felt when you delivered – or failed.

💬 WHAT I TELL MY TEAMS

- "Service is our brand in motion."
- "Every moment is a trust builder or a reputation leak."
- "Clients don't want perfect; they want present."
- "Don't solve. Elevate."
- "Make it unforgettable and make it *human*."

✍ FIELD NOTES

- Service isn't a reaction; it's a rhythm.
- The best clients aren't retained; they're cared for.
- Speed builds satisfaction. Presence builds trust.
- A missed expectation creates emotional drift, while a follow-up realigns it.
- Your culture is only real if your frontline carries it under pressure.

🔍 BEHIND THE CHAPTER

This chapter came into being after losing a major client I was certain we'd have for life. There were no major failures, no pricing disputes and no technical breakdowns. There was just a feeling that we weren't really *there* any more.

After they left, I reviewed every interaction, and the pattern was clear:

- We were slower than usual.
- Our tone was colder.
- Our follow-up was inconsistent.
- There were no surprises. No extra effort was made. Only silence.

That client didn't leave because we failed; they left because they felt *unseen*.

It was a moment that reshaped everything I thought I'd understood about service – not as a function, but as a cultural mirror. If your clients feel like they don't matter, then it doesn't matter how good your product is.

Losing that client was a hard pill to swallow, but it was a valuable reminder that service must be a cornerstone of leadership within my companies. We track it, train for it and rehearse it because it defines us.

We don't do it by using slogans and lofty promises, but through tone, timing and recovery. This chapter wasn't about solving problems. It was about building brand advocates who inspire loyalty from our clients.

RAISE THE STANDARD

- Where in your client journey have you over-automated the human touch?
- What's one emotional repair moment you've missed, and how can you rebuild it?
- Where can your team follow up *after* the problem is fixed, to deepen trust?
- What small, intentional surprise could elevate your client experience this week?

In the next chapter, we move from how you serve others to how you sustain yourself. We also explore why discipline, not motivation, separates leaders who drift from leaders who last.

NOTES

CHAPTER 24

DISCIPLINE OVER MOTIVATION

Motivation starts things. Discipline finishes them.

STRATEGIC INSIGHT

Motivation is temporary. Anyone can feel fired up when the vision is fresh, the results visible and the energy high. But the novelty wears off and the applause dies down, and when it does, most people stop putting energy into what they were doing – not because they're incapable or lazy, but because they built their consistency on mood, not muscle. Discipline doesn't wait to feel ready. It moves in silence, without applause. It doesn't spike; it compounds. It's the quiet engine behind reputations that last and brands that deliver long after the hype dies down. Discipline builds consistency, and consistency builds trust. It's how you keep showing up when everyone else has left the room.

THE MOMENT IT HIT ME: HOW DISCIPLINE CHANGED MY LIFE

During my tapering process from opioid addiction, there were no motivational speeches or biohacks wrapped in positive slogans. There was just discipline and structure.

I kept showing up when I least wanted to. I stuck to the tapering schedule. I trained when I was exhausted. I fuelled my body when I had no appetite. I led my companies through strategy sessions while privately managing excruciating pain.

It wasn't glamorous or Instagram-worthy, but every day, I made one decision: Do what needs to be done, especially when you don't feel like it.

That difficult time in my life didn't build hype; it built habits. And those habits are the same ones that helped me lead billion-rand businesses, stay healthy in my forties and finish what many people only start.

MINDSET PRINCIPLE: WHAT DISCIPLINE REALLY IS

- It's the decision you keep after the emotion is gone.
- It's doing the work when no one's watching.
- It's choosing alignment over excitement.
- It's building momentum by moving, especially when you don't feel like it.

Discipline is *emotional integrity*. It's how you stay loyal to your future even when your mood is stuck in the past.

FRAMEWORK/PLAYBOOK: HOW I DESIGN FOR DISCIPLINE

I Remove Emotion from Commitment.
I don't ask, "Do I feel like doing this?" I ask, "Did I say I would?" It's the only filter that matters.

I Create Non-Negotiables.

There are things I do daily without debate, not just "if I'm in the mood". I commit to:

- Waking up early
- Moving my body
- Eating clean
- Protecting energy
- Finishing what I promised

These aren't simply routines; they're also identity builders.

I Align My Environment With My Standards.

I commit to:

- Prepped meals
- Protected mornings
- No notifications during creation time
- A calendar built around energy, not just availability

I Track Completion, Not Motivation.

At the end of the day, I care less about how I felt and more about what I *finished*.

I Respect Resistance.

When resistance shows up, I don't flinch – I double down. Because it usually signals the exact thing I need to push through next.

⚠ WARNING SIGN: THE PROBLEM WITH MOTIVATION CULTURE

- It tricks you into waiting for the right moment.
- It makes you question everything the second discomfort shows up.
- It glorifies inspiration but abandons execution.

Worst of all, **it convinces you that discipline is punishment, when it's actually power.**

💭 WHAT I TELL MY TEAMS

- "We don't rely on mood. We rely on movement."
- "Motivation might get you started. Discipline makes you credible."
- "You're not here to feel ready. You're here to be reliable."
- "Success is scheduled, not sparked."
- "We don't skip the boring reps. We build with them."

✍ FIELD NOTES

- Discipline is identity in motion.
- What you do when no one's clapping is what defines you when the lights come on.
- You'll never feel like it all the time. That's why structure matters.
- The most elite brands are powered by boring, consistent decisions.
- You don't need another high. You need habits that hold.

🔍 BEHIND THE CHAPTER

I wrote this chapter on a day when I didn't feel like writing. I was drained, unmotivated and tired. The deadline was looming, and for a moment I questioned whether any of this mattered. But I sat down to write anyway. And when I was done, I wasn't drained. I was clear and calm.

That's when I was reminded once again that discipline isn't about being hard on yourself. It's about being aligned with who you said you'd be.

Discipline is what helped me to rebuild myself after my crash. It saved me during recovery and led me through pain and fatigue. The truth is, the people who win in the long term don't wait for motivation or hype. They rely on the habits they *manufacture* through mindset and structure.

📝 RAISE THE STANDARD

- Where are you still relying on motivation to stay consistent?
- What commitment needs to be protected, regardless of how you feel this week?
- What's one action you can take daily, no matter your mood?
- If your reputation was built only on what you finished, what would you change today?

In the next chapter, we explore what happens when the rhythm is broken, and how real leadership emerges when consistency is no longer enough.

NOTES

CHAPTER 25

LEADING THROUGH CRISIS

Pressure doesn't create leaders. It reveals them.

STRATEGIC INSIGHT

Most leaders look capable when things are calm, the markets are up, morale is high, their clients are loyal and their momentum is smooth. But leadership isn't proven in clear skies; it's revealed in a storm. Crisis doesn't care how clever you are or what title you hold. It only cares what you do next. Crisis doesn't test your plan; it exposes your foundation. And in that exposure, the real question emerges: Do you disappear when the going gets rough or do you stay and ride out the storm?

In the midst of a storm, the people around you don't need perfection. They need your presence. They need *you*.

THE MOMENT IT HIT ME: WHEN I HAD TO LEAD OR LOSE IT ALL

There have been moments in my career when everything was on the line – financially, emotionally and reputationally. But one incident stands out from the rest.

It was 2007. I had taken a R100-million bond from Standard Bank to develop a block of flats called Mont Blanc Heights, the biggest project to date that I'd ever attempted. We bonded everything: the business, our homes and all our assets. If we missed the completion deadline, the repayments would spike to R700 000 a month. If we defaulted, we'd lose it all.

There was no room for error. I lived on site and worked through the night. We met deadlines by hours, not days.

When a municipal inspector stalled over a parking-bay violation, I somehow managed to make the call that got us over the line. That December, we filed with the Deeds Office, hours before they closed for the festive season.

The property market crashed a few weeks later, in 2008. This wasn't a period of "business as usual"; it was about us teetering on the edge of a global crisis. We avoided losing everything by a couple of weeks.

During that time, I realised that leadership under pressure isn't about being perfect. It's about not panicking, and about being present, decisive, disciplined and fully accountable.

MINDSET PRINCIPLE: WHAT CRISIS LEADERSHIP ACTUALLY REQUIRES

Clarity Over Certainty

You don't need to know everything, but you need to be clear on what matters now – and what comes next.

Presence Over Perfection

Your team isn't looking for a saviour; they're looking for someone who shows up and *stays*. So, be there, be calm and be steady, even when you don't feel steady.

Speed Over Silence

Silence creates panic. Even a partial plan is better than invisible leadership. Move. Speak. Adjust in motion.

Empathy Over Ego

In times of crisis, some people get scared and some get angry. Your job isn't to overrule their emotions but to hold space for them.

Standards Over Emotion

Emotions fluctuate, but standards don't. When the storm hits, your people need something to hold on to. That anchor is the culture you've already built – the one you now reinforce.

🛠 FRAMEWORK/PLAYBOOK: MY FIVE-POINT CRISIS PLAYBOOK

Activate the 72-Hour Rule.

In the first three days, we:

- Acknowledge the reality
- Define the next moves
- Assign ownership
- Communicate clearly, internally and externally

Run an Energy Audit.

We ask:

- Who's frozen?
- Who's fuelling fear?
- Who's steady?

Calm is contagious. So is chaos.

Stabilise the Core.

Don't try to fix everything. Protect your most valuable people, your most fragile systems and your top-tier clients.

Reset Expectations, Not Standards.

Timelines may shift, but values stay locked in.

Overcommunicate the Vision.

Remind people why we're here, what we believe and what we're building through the crisis. When the outcome is blurry, your leadership and standards become the anchor.

⚠️ WARNING SIGN: WHAT HAPPENS WHEN YOU DON'T LEAD

- Silence becomes fear.
- Delays become mistrust.
- Micro-drama becomes macro-drift.
- Your team starts to guess, and they usually guess wrong.
- Crisis doesn't wait for you to be ready. Indecision is a decision.

WHAT I TELL MY TEAMS

- “This didn’t happen *to* us. It happened *for* our refinement.”
- “Calm is your superpower.”
- “Lead louder than the fear, but listen softer than the ego.”
- “Standards don’t shake. People do. So, hold the line.”
- “When others freeze, we move.”

FIELD NOTES

- You don’t need all the answers; you need *presence*.
- Leadership in crisis is about rhythm, not about rescue.
- Move first. Communicate fast. Then refine in motion.
- If you’re silent, the story gets written without you.
- The calmest voice leads, even when the facts are still forming.

BEHIND THE CHAPTER

Crisis isn’t theoretical to me. I’ve made payroll with hours to spare. I’ve begged banks for a lifeline and mortgaged everything I owned to finish something I believed in. But, no matter what, I’ve always shown up to lead, even when all I wanted to do was shut down.

And here’s what I’ve learned through every high-pressure moment: Your team doesn’t need you to be superhuman; they just need you to *be there*. They need you to hold the standard, both in the outcome and in the tone. They also need you to remind them, through your actions, your posture and your voice, that you won’t disappear in the storm.

This chapter isn't for your best day. It's for the day when everything feels like it might fall apart, because that's when real leadership begins.

RAISE THE STANDARD

- Where have you gone quiet when your team needs your voice?
- What fear is draining your culture right now, and how will you address it?
- What's the single most important action you can take in the next 72 hours to stabilise your leadership?
- Are you reacting to pressure or upholding your standard?

In the next chapter, we move from leading under pressure to protecting the culture that outlives it. Then we explore what happens when culture is either compounded or silently slips away.

NOTES

CHAPTER 26

PROTECTING THE CULTURE AT ALL COSTS

The culture you don't control, controls you.

STRATEGIC INSIGHT

Culture doesn't collapse overnight. It corrodes quietly when leaders stop reinforcing it. You can't pause culture – it's being reinforced or rewritten every day through what's allowed, repeated and ignored. And if you're not leading it intentionally, someone else's tone will lead it for you.

THE MOMENT IT HIT ME: A LEADERSHIP WAKE-UP CALL

In 2016, I began taking my motorcycle racing seriously. I was training at the racetrack during the week, chasing milliseconds and obsessed with the craft.

What I didn't realise was that while I was focused on speed, things inside my business were quietly spiralling. I had stepped back from the operational frontline and handed more authority to senior staff. On paper, they were capable, but in practice, their leadership was untested – and it showed.

What started as subtle power struggles turned into open conflict. Managers dragged their teams into the tension. Meetings turned political. Decisions turned personal. People stopped collaborating. Departments protected their turf. The atmosphere was tense, and staff feared each other more than they feared our competitors. Dismissals rose, and resignations followed.

And it was my fault. I'd built the business, but I hadn't protected the culture.

That was the moment I realised: You can't race ahead if the wheels behind you are falling off.

🧠 MINDSET PRINCIPLE: HOW CULTURE COMPOUNDS OR CRACKS

Culture is compounded through:

- Clear standards
- Shared language
- Consistent feedback
- Reinforced alignment
- Daily behavioural proof

Culture cracks through:

- Silent tolerance
- Weak onboarding
- Energy drift
- Inconsistent leadership
- Standards that go uncorrected

🛠 FRAMEWORK/PLAYBOOK: HOW I REINFORCE CULTURE EVERY DAY

We Script the Standard.

Nothing is left to chance. We document what "exceptional" looks like by:

- How we speak to clients
- How we respond to tension
- How we hand off work
- How we protect energy

If it matters, it's taught – but it's never assumed.

We Rehearse Culture Weekly, Not Yearly.

Cultural reminders don't wait for retreats or events. They show up in:

- Weekly wins
- Micro-shoutouts
- Morning stand-ups
- Post-mortems

We Front-Load Culture in Onboarding.

The first 30 days shape everything. We don't just teach people to use tools; we also install identity.

We Scale Through Culture Carriers.

I look for the people who:

- Hold the tone
- Spot the drift
- Reinforce the rhythm

Then I give them more voice, visibility and leadership responsibility.

We Kill Complacency Early On.

When I see someone drift, even slightly, I deal with it. One unchecked behaviour becomes everyone's new baseline.

⚠ WARNING SIGN: WHAT HAPPENS WHEN YOUR CULTURE ISN'T COMPOUNDED

- Standards drop
- Tone dulls
- Energy fades
- New hires drift faster
- Loyalty decays

By the time performance dips, the culture that once protected you is already gone. Culture doesn't fall apart loudly. It fades, and *then it fails*.

💬 WHAT I TELL MY TEAMS

- "Culture is built by what you allow, not just by what you say."
- "If we're not reinforcing it, we're rewriting it."
- "Every action is a culture vote."
- "Protect the rhythm. Protect the tone. Protect each other."
- "Drift doesn't scream; it silently slides."

✍ FIELD NOTES

- Culture is maintenance, not momentum.
- Every interaction either strengthens or weakens who you say you are.
- Culture never sleeps; it's compounded silently.
- Rituals protect identity. Silence rewrites it.
- If your culture isn't being reinforced, it's being rewritten.

BEHIND THE CHAPTER

I wrote this chapter after walking into a meeting where everything looked fine but nothing felt sharp. The team was aligned and the agenda clear, but the energy was flat. No one said anything wrong, yet the spark was gone. That's when it hit me: We'd stopped reinforcing the culture that built us. And that was on me. Because culture doesn't survive on memory; it survives on reinforcement.

This chapter isn't about what to do when everything is broken. It's about what to do when things feel just good enough to stop paying attention. Because the moment you stop feeding your culture, you start losing it.

RAISE THE STANDARD

- Where has culture drifted without anyone calling it?
- What behaviour are you tolerating that doesn't align with who you say you are?
- Who's carrying the culture right now, and how are you reinforcing their influence?
- What rhythm, ritual or reinforcement system needs to come back, starting this week?

In the next chapter, we redefine wealth not by what you keep but by what you activate. We then explore how you deploy what you've built in order to elevate others.

NOTES

CHAPTER 27

THE WEALTH MINDSET SHIFT

Wealth isn't just what you earn. It's also what you elevate.

STRATEGIC INSIGHT

There comes a point in the journey where money stops being the scoreboard. One day you realise that "more" isn't the ultimate goal any more.

You've bought the freedom, built the infrastructure and proven what you needed to prove. You've accumulated assets, built brands and grown your influence.

What really matters begins to shift. You start asking different questions: Who am I becoming? What am I building beyond myself? What is this wealth actually doing for others, not just for me? That's the moment the wealth mindset shifts from accumulation to activation, from ownership to impact and from control to contribution.

Because wealth isn't what you keep; it's what you *deploy*.

THE MOMENT IT HIT ME: THE DAY MY DEFINITION OF WEALTH CHANGED

One night, I was reviewing our financials. The numbers looked incredible, and the companies were thriving. The financial scoreboard looked exactly like I had once dreamed it would, but I didn't feel the satisfaction that I thought I'd feel. I wasn't excited; in fact, I felt flat.

That's when it hit me. I realised that I didn't need more money – I needed better questions. So, I asked myself, "Is this capital multiplying meaning or just sitting there?"

I wasn't chasing the wrong thing; I had just outgrown the metric. That's when I stopped chasing net worth and started focusing on net impact. It was a massive turning point.

MINDSET PRINCIPLE: THE REAL WEALTH SHIFT

Most people grow up with a transactional mindset about money. We're taught to hold on to as much as we can, spend as little as possible and prove that we've "made it" through what we accumulate. But true wealth isn't just about retention. It's also about how you release, deploy and reinvest.

For me, the mindset shift was about moving from "How much can I keep?" to "How much can I activate?" It was about realising that wealth isn't power – unless it's used to elevate something beyond yourself. And if your wealth dies with you, it was never truly wealth – it was storage.

🛠 FRAMEWORK/PLAYBOOK: HOW I SHIFTED INTO STRATEGIC WEALTH

The first thing I changed was how I filtered decisions. Every rand now has to answer a purpose-aligned question: Does this create freedom, future or legacy? If the answer is no, it's simply meaningless noise. If it's yes, it's power. This filter alone removed unnecessary spending and clarified where to channel my capital.

I also shifted my investments from paper ROI to what I now call ROH – return on humans. This means funding team development, mentoring high-potential leaders, investing in staff education and providing my family with equity of the emotional kind: time, presence and belief in them. If something multiplies people and legacy, I back it.

Generosity has also become a core strategy. It's not a side hobby or a tax write-off. It's a leadership lens. When I give time, clarity, frameworks or capital, it always comes back multiplied. I've come to believe that scarcity is expensive and abundance is strategic.

I have also started buying back time – time with my family, time to create and time to experience the life I've built. There's no point in building empires if you're not emotionally present in any of them. Now, if money can buy back presence, it's well spent.

Finally, I shifted my focus to building assets that outlive me. Not just property, but also people, systems, intellectual capital, culture and brand equity. For me, it's about a legacy that moves forward even when I'm no longer around.

⚠ WARNING SIGN: THE COST OF CHASING MORE WITHOUT MEANING

- You grow resentful of what you once wanted.
- You stay busy but feel flat.
- You succeed and still feel left behind.
- You measure life in assets, not in impact.
- Worst of all, you lose sight of *why you started building at all.*

WHAT I TELL MY TEAMS

- "Wealth isn't what you keep. It's what you enable."
- "Money grows when it flows with purpose."
- "Don't build to impress. Build to elevate."
- "Let your capital serve your calling."
- "The real flex? Freedom, presence and peace."

FIELD NOTES

- Wealth without impact is just accumulation.
- Buy back your energy, your creativity and your ability to build what matters.
- If your money isn't moving others forward, it's not working hard enough.
- True legacy is measured in people, not in possessions.
- The wealthiest leaders I know are the most generous with their time, trust and belief.

BEHIND THE CHAPTER

I wrote this chapter after watching a young team member I'd mentored, land a role he'd once thought was out of his reach. He'd come straight out of school with no additional qualifications, but he was consistent, committed and incredibly coachable. Watching him realise his own value was more meaningful than any asset I had acquired that year.

That's when it clicked. My personal balance sheet doesn't measure wealth. My true net worth is the trajectories of the people I've mentored and built up.

The wealth mindset shift doesn't happen when you cross a financial threshold. It happens when you stop asking what you're keeping and start asking what you're building.

RAISE THE STANDARD

- Where are you still measuring wealth by what you hold rather than by what you elevate?
- Who in your world could be multiplied if you deployed your resources differently?
- What would it look like to make generosity part of your operational strategy?
- If someone studied your capital flows, what would they say you truly value?

Now let's recap what you've learned in Part IV.

NOTES

🔁 PART IV RECAP – SCALING, LEGACY & IMPACT

Growth is what you build. Legacy is what you leave behind.

This section wasn't about expansion for expansion's sake. It was about meaningful scale – growth that's aligned, durable and deeply human. Because scale without culture fractures, service without heart fades and wealth without impact is simply accumulation in disguise.

Part IV pushed you to ask deeper questions:

- Who are you really serving?
- What systems are you reinforcing?
- Where are you deploying your resources, not just your energy?

Scaling isn't just about multiplying effort. It's about multiplying what matters.

📌 WHAT YOU'VE JUST MASTERED

Chapter 22: When Risk Pays Off

Risk isn't reckless; it's required. Progress starts when courage overtakes calculation. The cost of waiting is far greater than the cost of trying.

Chapter 23: The Customer Service Manifesto

Service is not a department. It's the brand in action. Every interaction earns or erodes trust.

Chapter 24: Discipline Over Motivation

Motivation fades. Discipline compounds. Consistency isn't just output; it's also who you become through the repetition of exceptional standards.

Chapter 25: Leading Through Crisis

Pressure reveals leadership. When the ground shakes, your team needs your calm, clarity and presence more than perfection.

Chapter 26: Protecting the Culture at All Costs

Culture never pauses. It either reinforces who you are or quietly rewrites what you tolerate.

Chapter 27: The Wealth Mindset Shift

Wealth isn't measured by what you keep but by what you deploy. Legacy lives in the people and systems you've built, not in your balance sheet.

YOUR LEGACY AUDIT: SIX QUESTIONS TO REFLECT ON

- Where are you mistaking performance for impact?
- What would your team protect if you weren't in the room?
- What's one risk you've avoided that's now costing you opportunity?
- What system, ritual or value needs to be reinforced before it fades?
- Who could rise if you shifted your time, trust or capital?
- If your influence ended tomorrow, what would live on in your business?

💥 THE SHIFT

You've built the standard, embedded the structure and created the energy. Now, the question is: What will it all mean if it doesn't outlive you?

This section wasn't about finishing strong. It was about scaling with depth, anchoring speed with soul and transforming capital into contribution. Because leadership isn't about how you show up when you're celebrated. It's about what remains when you're no longer around, and what still works without you.

In the next part, we close the loop and expand. Because building something extraordinary is about what you choose to protect when the pressure rises and the spotlight fades.

NOTES

PART V

EXPANSION & EXPOSURE

CHAPTER 28

THE COST OF COMPLACENCY

Drift doesn't happen loudly. It happens in silence and costs everything.

STRATEGIC INSIGHT

Most businesses don't collapse in a blaze; they collapse in silence. Things start falling apart when tolerance of "average" first slips in, a standard is missed and a compromise is made "just for now". No one notices the complacency until it's too late.

That's the danger of complacency. It doesn't feel like failure; it often feels like stability. That's until you realise you've drifted so far from your edge that the brand no longer resembles what you'd set out to build. And by the time you feel the change, **complacency has already rewritten your business.**

THE MOMENT IT HIT ME: THE DRIFT I ALMOST MISSED

There was a season in my insurance business when everything looked healthy on paper. Growth was solid, our clients were satisfied and team performance was steady.

But something was missing. Decisions took longer. Accountability blurred. Documents weren't as sharp as they should have been. The culture still functioned, but it no longer felt exceptional.

It took some time for me to realise that we had drifted from our own standard. No one had stopped caring, but they had also not noticed that we were slipping. We weren't failing, but we weren't rising either.

That's the problem with drift. You rarely see it in the numbers, but you feel it in the energy, the tone and the timing. It's in the pause before someone speaks and the silence when someone should have. And that's the most dangerous part of complacency – it *feels like nothing's wrong.*

MINDSET PRINCIPLE: WHAT DRIFT LOOKS LIKE IN REAL TIME

- "It's just one deadline we're missing."
- "It's not urgent."
- "The client won't notice."
- "This still kind of works. We'll improve it later."
- "We've always done it this way."

But drift doesn't keep to small slips or oversights. Eventually:

- Talent disengages.
- Clients question value.
- Culture softens.
- Execution loses its edge.

Suddenly, what you built no longer resembles what you intended.

🛠 FRAMEWORK/PLAYBOOK: HOW I CATCH DRIFT BEFORE IT IS COMPOUNDED

I Audit Energy Weekly.

Culture shows up in posture, tone and timing, not just in metrics. If the energy in a room is flat, I dig deeper before performance starts reflecting the problem.

I Recalibrate the Standard Out Loud.

Every quarter, we ask:

- What are we tolerating that used to be non-negotiable?
- What's become "fine" that was once exceptional?

I Call the Small Before It Becomes Big.

One sloppy email, one poor handover or one missed moment: I don't let it slide. I flag it immediately and constructively.

I Reset Rhythm, Not Just Metrics.

When drift appears, we don't just measure harder. We *move better*. We clarify meetings, rebuild systems and make speed a priority again.

⚠ WARNING SIGN: WHY MOST LEADERS MISS IT

Because drift feels like safety, we are often seduced by the false idea that:

- "Things are working."
- "No one's complaining."
- "It's not broken yet."

But here's the truth: **Complacency doesn't feel dangerous until the fallout makes you wish you'd paid attention earlier.**

💬 WHAT I TELL MY LEADERS

- "Nothing just happens. It was tolerated first."
- "If it feels slightly off, speak up."
- "Drift is the tax you pay for quiet compromise."
- "Complacency doesn't ask permission. It waits for silence."
- "Don't wait for the fire. Watch for the flicker."

✍ FIELD NOTES

- Gradual decline doesn't shout; it whispers.
- The brand doesn't break all at once. It erodes quietly, one small tolerance at a time.
- Every silent "It's fine" becomes a defining vote for mediocrity.
- Drift never feels urgent until you realise you're far from where you started.
- If no one has noticed the standards slipping, the erosion is already advanced.

🔍 BEHIND THE CHAPTER

I wrote this chapter after sitting in a meeting where everything looked impressive but something felt off. The room was too quiet, the tone too safe and the answers too smooth. No one thing was wrong, but nothing felt sharp. Around the same time, we were hit with the largest fire claim we'd ever had. It wasn't just a tough loss – it was a wake-up call. The client should never have been underwritten without a full understanding of the risks. We hadn't been reckless, but we had been complacent.

That claim forced us to build what we should've built sooner: a full-service risk-management division and a disciplined onboarding system. Drift had exposed our blind spot, and the cost of complacency nearly broke us.

That near-catastrophe taught us that drift isn't a decision; it's the absence of one. And if you don't confront it in time, you'll pay for it later, with compound interest.

📝 RAISE THE STANDARD

- What's quietly drifting in your business while you focus on louder problems?
- Where have you started accepting "just okay" because it hasn't broken yet?
- What's one standard you need to recalibrate out loud this week?
- What early signal have you felt recently but not acted on?

In the next chapter, we explore why the people who lead with transparency build belief in businesses that scale new heights.

NOTES

CHAPTER 29

BUILDING IN PUBLIC

Your journey is the brand, not just the result.

STRATEGIC INSIGHT

There was a time when leaders stayed silent until a project was completed. They waited until their product was polished, the design flawless and the outcome guaranteed.

But the world has changed.

Today, the people who lead with the most impact are those who lead with exposure. They let others witness the process. They document the build. They teach through transparency. They don't wait for perfection before they share. They let people see what it looks like to refine out loud. **Today, trust is built through exposure – not just through execution.**

That's the power of building in public – not for attention but for alignment.

🔥 THE MOMENT IT HIT ME: WHEN I STOPPED HIDING THE PROCESS

For years, I believed showing vulnerability would weaken my authority and that sharing the mess behind closed doors would dilute the brand. I believed that only the wins should be visible. But that thinking changed when I started sharing my personal flaws and challenges.

To my surprise, people didn't lose trust in me when I opened up about my battle with addiction, when I showed the behind-the-scenes of the gym build, when I spoke honestly about leadership fatigue and burnout, and when I let the team into the moments I used to hide.

Instead, they leaned in.

They saw the human behind the vision, and suddenly, the brand scaled and the relationships inside the company deepened. Trust multiplied because the challenges felt shared. When people see the truth, they feel included in the mission – not just marketed to.

🧠 MINDSET PRINCIPLE: WHY BUILDING IN PUBLIC BUILDS BELIEF

- It deepens trust.
- It teaches through process.
- It creates emotional equity.
- It invites alignment.
- It makes you *real*.

People don't follow perfection. They follow consistency and clarity, and they follow builders who are *honest about the process of evolving*.

🛠️ FRAMEWORK/PLAYBOOK: HOW I BUILD IN PUBLIC WITHOUT OVERSHARING

I Share the Process, Not Just the Product.

When we launch something, we also share:

- What broke
- What we fixed
- What we learned
- What's coming next

People don't only see the end; they see the evolution too.

I Document Lessons in Motion.

I write the following in real time, not only after it's all been polished:

- Internal memos
- Voice notes
- Staff debriefs
- Public posts

These aren't wrapped in pretty bows. They're shared while they're still raw.

I Show Gratitude, Not Just Achievement.

Every milestone I share includes the people who made it possible:

- Team shoutouts
- Partner recognition
- Client appreciation

When you build in public, it's not about ego. It's about honouring the ecosystem.

I Protect the Sacred but Share the Strategic.
I don't share everything. Some things must stay private, but if it can help, guide or inspire others, I share it fully and generously.

⚠ WARNING SIGN: WHAT HAPPENS WHEN YOU ONLY SHOW THE END

- People disconnect from your process.
- Clients feel like outsiders.
- Staff think leadership is simply luck and polish.
- The brand feels distant, even if it's impressive.

If you only share what's finished, you lose the *emotional equity* of what got you there.

💬 WHAT I TELL MY BUILDERS

- "Let people see the scaffolding, not just the skyline."
- "Share your version one. Own it. Then improve it out loud."
- "People don't connect with perfection. They connect with process."
- "Progress shared is belief multiplied."
- "If you hide the build, you hide the brand."
- "Your scars don't make you weak. They make you real."
- "Transparency is the new marketing."
- "What you show, shapes what people remember."

✍ FIELD NOTES

- Your story isn't what you've built. It's what you've *built through*.
- Exposure isn't weakness. It's leadership with the ego removed.
- People follow process, not just product.
- Vulnerability earns trust when paired with structure.
- The mission becomes movement when others see it unfolding in real time.

🔍 BEHIND THE CHAPTER

I wrote this chapter after a client said, "I trust your brand because you've never pretended it's perfect."

That remark stuck with me because it reminded me that when you build in public, people don't just watch you win – they watch you *become*. And, more importantly, they feel part of it.

These days, I build publicly on purpose – not for applause and validation but for *alignment*. Because alignment outlasts attention, and exposure doesn't just build connection – it also builds *legacy*.

RAISE THE STANDARD

- Where are you hiding the process that could actually inspire belief?
- What story are you holding back because it's still unfinished?
- What lesson could your team, market or ecosystem learn from your current challenge?
- What would change if your leadership became more visible, not just more polished?

In the next chapter, we close the book on performance and open the door to how you're seen when the building stops and your reputation is birthed.

NOTES

CHAPTER 30

YOUR NAME IS THE STANDARD

If it carries your name, it carries your reputation.

STRATEGIC INSIGHT

I don't care if it's a quote, a proposal, a customer reply, a table, a deck, a menu or a floor tile – if it carries your name, it carries your reputation.

This is the chapter where we stop pretending excellence is optional and where we stop accepting "good enough" in the name of speed and efficiency. It's the point where we stop tolerating what we'd never sign if our signatures were on the page.

Because if you're the builder, the leader or the visionary, then your name is the brand. **Your name is on everything – whether it's printed there or not.** It's on every detail and every handover. It's in the tone and in the last 10% of execution that no one else but you would notice.

How you show up in the smallest details is how the world learns to trust the big ones.

THE MOMENT IT HIT ME: WHEN I FELT THE STANDARD SLIP

In the early years of the business, we didn't have a staff uniform. Everyone dressed however they liked. At the time, I didn't think it mattered. We were growing, and people were working hard. The energy felt good, so I let it slide.

But one morning, I walked into our office and saw what was really happening. One team member was wearing gym gear, while another looked like they were dressed for a night out on the town. Some sported creased T-shirts; others just didn't look like they cared much.

No one had done anything intentionally wrong, but collectively, we looked completely unprofessional and untidy rather than premium or serious.

In that moment, I realised that it was my fault. I had built the business but not protected the standard.

I then understood: If it carries my name, it reflects my values. And if I tolerate the small things, I quietly rewrite the message.

The next day, I changed everything. We introduced a dress code, not to create clones or control but to create alignment. Because when people dress with pride, they show up with presence. That was the day I decided: If my name is on it, it had better look, feel and behave like it matters.

🧠 MINDSET PRINCIPLE: WHAT IT MEANS TO MAKE YOUR NAME THE STANDARD

- You notice what others ignore.
- You raise what others lower.
- You lead even when you're not visible.
- You act like *every detail* is a brand message – because it is.

This isn't about ego; it's about *craftsmanship*. Because your name is your legacy, and every careless decision you tolerate or sign off on becomes part of it.

🛠 FRAMEWORK/PLAYBOOK: HOW I DESIGN WITH MY NAME IN MIND

I Ask, "Would I Be Proud to Sign This?"

If the answer is no, it's not ready – no matter how small or how urgent it is.

I Imagine My Kids Walking Into It.

If I wouldn't want Dino or Gabby to see it and say, "My father built this," it gets fixed on the spot.

I Treat Anonymous Work Like Autographed Work.

Even if no one sees my fingerprint, *I see it*. And that's more than enough to make sure it's exceptional.

I Make Reputation the First Filter.

We don't just ask, "Is it done?" We ask, "Does this reflect what we stand for?" Because you can't scale trust without standard.

⚠ WARNING SIGN: WHY THIS CHAPTER MATTERS

You can outsource marketing and operations. You can even delegate parts of leadership, but you cannot outsource accountability. Your name is on everything, even when no one but you sees it.

💬 WHAT I TELL MY TEAMS

- "Would you put your name on this?"
- "Your name isn't just on the wall; it's in all the details."
- "Every touchpoint is a silent signature."
- "If you wouldn't let your family experience it, don't expose your client to it."
- "What you choose to ignore becomes your new standard."

✍ FIELD NOTES

- Your name is your final layer of quality control.
- What you tolerate will one day define you.
- Reputation isn't printed. It's *felt.*
- If you built it, it reflects you, whether you like it or not.
- Your legacy is hiding in the details you almost ignored.

🔍 BEHIND THE CHAPTER

I wrote this chapter after walking into one of our office spaces that had our logo on the wall but lacked our standard in the room. The detail wasn't sharp. The vibe wasn't intentional.

We looked like a business that had grown quickly but not intentionally. We looked messy. And I realised that it was on me. Because your logo might be on the wall, but your leadership lives in the atmosphere.

So, I changed it. I introduced a dress code and reset the tone. Now, I don't just inspect execution. I ask myself one question: Would I sign this with my name? And if the answer is no, it gets redone.

📝 RAISE THE STANDARD

- What detail in your business would make you hesitate to sign your name under it?
- Where has the standard quietly dropped because no one reinforced it?
- What would happen if your signature was required for every client experience this week?
- What's one corner you've tolerated that now needs to reflect your name again?

In the next chapter, I write a letter to all hardworking builders at all the different stages of their journeys.

NOTES

CHAPTER 31

A LETTER TO ALL THE BUILDERS

You don't need to follow the blueprint.

This chapter is written for you, the builder, to help you create something unique, enduring and exceptional at every stage of your journey.

To the Builder at the Beginning:

Maybe it's your first venture, your first risk or your first time leading others. You're probably excited but unsure whether anyone will believe in what you're creating. That's normal. You are not supposed to feel ready at the outset. My advice is simple: Just start. Don't wait for permission, applause or market validation. Build before anyone else believes in you. If no one sees it yet, believe louder. Because you were not made to fit in or wait to be chosen. You don't need a title to lead. Make mistakes. Own them. Learn fast. Protect your integrity like it's the most valuable thing you own – because it is.

To the Builder in Battle:

You're scaling under pressure, leading through complexity and carrying more than anyone realises. You've proven that you can build, but you are tired and stretched. You might be wondering if the cost is still worth it. I can reassure you that it is, but only if you build from alignment, not from exhaustion.

Don't chase growth that drains your spirit. Don't protect a machine that no longer serves your mission. Pause if you must, and recalibrate. Your team doesn't need your perfection. They need your presence, your clarity and your standard.

To the Builder Who's Burnt Out:
You've done what few would dare to attempt. You've held the vision, protected the brand and delivered again and again. But now you feel nothing. You're numb, exhausted and disconnected from the very thing you once lived for.

Let me be clear: You don't owe anyone your burnout. The world does not need more exhausted leaders. It needs recovered builders who rise again, not to impress but to build better. I've been there. And I can tell you with certainty, you can rest without quitting and recover without disappearing. You can rebuild your identity and your standard without losing your credibility. Take time out. Rest. Then return stronger.

To My Children, Dino And Gabby, and to Every Young Leader:

I wrote this book for you – not to give you answers but to show you what it means to build with your name on every detail and to lead with integrity.

You don't have to chase titles. You don't have to wait to be chosen. Build what others won't. Say what others are afraid to. And most of all, lead like what you are building will outlive you, because it will. You don't need to follow the blueprint. You *are* the blueprint.

Before we get to my final words, let's recap what you've learned in Part V.

NOTES

🔁 PART V RECAP – EXPANSION & EXPOSURE

Your growth isn't only measured by what you build but also by what you're willing to protect, expose and sign your name to.

At this level, leadership isn't about scaling faster; it's about deepening trust, exposing the process and defending the standard.

Part V closed the loop between internal precision and external perception. It reminded us that the world doesn't just follow what we say; it follows what we show, what we tolerate and what we're willing to put our name on.

This section spelled out three core truths:

- Drift happens silently, and costs everything if left unchecked.
- People connect more with process than with perfection, and building in public multiplies belief.
- Your name isn't just on the wall. It's also in the energy, the detail and the tone of every touchpoint that represents you.

Part V wasn't about reaching more people or getting more clients. It was about being more accountable to the ones who already believe in what you've built.

📌 WHAT YOU'VE JUST MASTERED

Chapter 28: The Cost of Complacency

Drift doesn't scream; it slides. And by the time you notice the damage, the erosion is already deep.

Chapter 29: Building in Public

Transparency builds trust faster than polish and glamour ever can. Process shared is belief multiplied.

Chapter 30: Your Name Is the Standard

If it reflects your name, it reflects your identity. And the smallest detail often carries the loudest legacy.

Chapter 31: A Letter to All the Builders

Legacy isn't built in hindsight. It's built in how you lead today, whether you're starting, scaling, rebuilding or mentoring those who will go further than you ever did.

YOUR FINAL LEADERSHIP AUDIT

- What have you been tolerating quietly that would damage your reputation if it was made public?
- Where are you overestimating the strength of a standard you no longer reinforce?
- What could you share in public this month to multiply belief in what you're building?
- If someone evaluated your leadership purely on tone, rhythm and repetition, what would they learn?
- What are you signing silently through inaction?

💥 THE SHIFT

This section wasn't about exposure for attention. It was about exposure for accountability.

You've done the internal work and built the systems. What matters now is how those systems show up when no one's watching, and what your reputation carries when you're no longer in the room.

Leadership at this level is no longer about potential. It's about what's visible, consistent and enforced, because the standard is no longer just something you build.

It's something you carry.

NOTES

FINAL WORD

Slay the standard: Carry it, raise it, slay it.

You haven't reached the end of this book by accident. You got here because something in you refused to let complacency win. You made it through every chapter, every uncomfortable reflection in the mirror and every hard truth. For that, I congratulate you. But don't mistake it for a trophy to admire and shelve, because this book is a toolkit, a weapon, a warning and a field manual. It was forged under pressure, in the trenches and in challenging seasons that demanded more from me than I ever thought I had to give. I didn't write it to impress anyone; I wrote it because the world is drowning in noise and starving for clarity.

I've seen what happens when talented people lower their standards just once, in the name of survival. I've seen great brands lose their edge, cultures lose their soul and leaders disappear into performance theatre, not because they lacked talent but because they stopped carrying the weight that leadership demands.

I've been there. I've led through addiction and withdrawals. My businesses have run on empty. I've expanded while nearly collapsing. I've lost clarity. I've tolerated mediocrity. I've had to rebuild not just companies but also my entire identity.

But from the ashes, I've learned how to build differently. I've learned to build systems that outlive me, cultures that protect what I value and teams that lead without waiting for permission.

Leadership isn't about being the loudest or the smartest. It's about whether your standard still speaks long after you've left the room. Because real builders finish what others only start.

Everything I've built – in insurance, fitness, hospitality and motorsport – has come down to one non-negotiable: Raise the standard.

Therefore, this book is a challenge to you, your team, your business and everything you claim to care about. Because if *Slaying the Standard* has taught you anything, it's this: the standard isn't a slogan; it's a system, and it's either enforced or erased. So now that we've come to the end of the book, only one question remains: Will you carry the standard?

As I have constantly reminded you, drift is real. Distraction is constant. The easiest thing in the world is to lower the bar just once and convince yourself it's only temporary. But what you lower once, you begin to accept. What you accept, you start to repeat. And what you repeat becomes who you are – your culture, your brand and your legacy.

That's why this book doesn't end with a conclusion but with a decision. You need to decide whether you will keep tolerating what you've quietly let slide or whether you will raise the bar for good. Will you stop managing chaos and start protecting clarity? Will you no longer chase momentum but start multiplying mastery? You need to decide whether you're going to stop waiting to be ready and start leading like it already matters – because it does.

So, here's my final suggestion. Don't just close this book. Use it. Let it shape how you speak, hire, design and lead. Let it whisper to you and remind you when you drift. Let it confront you when you slip. Let it raise your hand when no one else will. Let it live in every boardroom and backroom you enter, without you needing to say a word.

Because one day, no one will remember the revenue you helped them make. They won't remember the systems, the slides or the spreadsheets. They'll remember how it felt to be led by you. They'll remember what you built, what you protected and what you refused to tolerate. They'll remember the weight of your expectations, the clarity of your vision and the culture you left behind.

They'll remember the standard you set.

So, don't close this book and go back to normal. Close it and begin again, differently, deliberately and without apology.

Build like it matters, because it does. Lead like it lasts, because it must. And raise the standard, not once but every single day, until the people around you do the same without having to be asked.

Because the standard isn't just what you expect. It's what you enforce, what you embody and what you leave behind.

And when in doubt, remember this:

You are the standard now.

So, carry it, raise it, slay it.